LETTERS TO A
YOUNG CHEF

ALSO BY DANIEL BOULUD

Cooking with Daniel Boulud

Café Boulud Cookbook:
French-American Recipes for the Home Cook

Chef Daniel Boulud: Cooking in New York City
with Peter Kaminsky

Daniel's Dish: Entertaining at Home with a Four-Star Chef

Braise: A Journey Through International Cuisine
with Melissa Clark

Cocktails & Amuse-Bouches: For Her & For Him

Daniel: My French Cuisine
with Sylvie Bigar

My Best: Daniel Boulud

LETTERS TO A
YOUNG CHEF

—◆—

DANIEL BOULUD

BASIC BOOKS
New York

Basic Books
Hachette Book Group
1290 Avenue of the Americas, New York, NY 10104
www.basicbooks.com
Printed in the United States of America

Originally published in hardcover by Basic Books in August 2003

Second Trade Paperback Edition: October 2017

Published by Basic Books, an imprint of Perseus Books, LLC, a subsidiary of Hachette Book Group, Inc.

The Hachette Speakers Bureau provides a wide range of authors for speaking events. To find out more, go to www.hachettespeakersbureau.com or call (866) 376-6591.

The publisher is not responsible for websites (or their content) that are not owned by the publisher.

Print book interior design by Jeff Williams.

Library of Congress Control Number: 2017941855

ISBNs: 978-0-465-00735-6 (hardcover); 978-0-465-00777-6 (2007 paperback); 978-0-465-09342-7 (2017 paperback); 978-0-7867-3661-4 (e-book)

LSC-C

Printing 4, 2021

*To Julien et Julien, my father and my son,
who represent both the best of my past and all
the joy and promise of the future. And to the
countless young chefs who work hard to succeed
with creativity and taste while preserving
the traditions of their cuisine.*

CONTENTS

—◆—

CONTENTS

A FEW LETTERS FROM MY FRIENDS

INTRODUCTION

MUCH HAS CHANGED since I first wrote these letters fifteen years ago. Some things haven't, though; carrots are still carrots, and a roast chicken is much as it was in my grandmother's day (and in her grandmother's as well). You need the same knife skills now that I learned as a young apprentice, and it will take you the same amount of time to master them. We live in a world where social media has brought every chef into instant contact with his or her peers and family, and with clientele from all around the world. Serve a bad meal tonight and thousands of social media users will know about it by morning. Serve a great one and food enthusiasts will start clamoring for reservations. Invent a new recipe in Paris tonight and it may be imitated in Los Angeles tomorrow.

Perhaps not exactly tomorrow, because no matter how fast information moves, it still takes time to figure out how to break down a recipe and master the steps necessary to turn it from a good idea to a practical item on the menu. The appetite for change has accelerated, but meeting the challenge of quality and consistency means that the successful chefs move only as fast as the capabilities of their staff, the reliability of their purveyors, and the tastes of their customers.

We swim in a rising sea of information among an ever more informed public that is always on the hunt for the next hot trend. Staying good and staying interesting are constant challenges, much more so today than just a few years ago. Add to this the unreality of food television that features frantic competition, weird combinations of ingredients, and a jury of experts providing instant, often brutal, criticism. As successful as these shows are, they have fostered a less than realistic conception of what it takes to be a chef. Yes, speed is important, but never at the expense of accuracy. And although a good chef is often called upon to improvise when ingredients vary in quality and availability, a true chef is known more by his or her consistently high level of execution than by the ability to throw random ingredients together. Some of the candidates on the shows certainly have a lot of talent, but what's portrayed is not always true to the reality of working in a restaurant. It's much more about good TV than it is about good cooking. Having said that, I've participated in judging on those shows. I'm like the rest of you: I watch the programs and often enjoy them. Cooking shows have always been very entertaining media for all generations and will remain so; I simply caution aspiring young cooks against glamorizing them too much.

Perhaps the two most important waves of innovation in the last decades have come from the Spanish and the Scandinavians. In Spain twenty years ago, Ferran Adrià spearheaded a technological revolution that inspired many chefs to try their hands at new textures, tastes, and methods, often using foams, gels, colloids, and other substances and tools better known in the food laboratory than in a conventional kitchen. The results of the modernist molecular gastronomy movement were tastes, textures, and shapes that delighted, entranced, and mystified (in a good way). But in the hands of less accomplished chefs, the movement also resulted in some strange and unsatisfying food, sacrificed at the altar of novelty. At Restaurant DANIEL we've adopted some of those techniques—I'm not opposed to them. I just think they should not be done recklessly, but rather with purpose and always in balance.

At the opposite, northern end of Europe, René Redzepi and his cosigners of the Nordic Manifesto encouraged us to look to the humble, often overlooked ingredients that could be foraged from the forests, oceans, fields, and lakes right outside our door, wherever that door might be. We have seen the same ethic in a different style with the geolocality of ingredients used in the regional cooking of France, Italy, or any nutrient-rich region, but never before to the extreme of finding less obvious ingredients the way Redzepi has done. I believe this is going to be a growing and long-term trend that will widen our knowledge of ingredients and open us to the possibilities of rediscovering flavors and textures known to our distant ancestors but that have been passed by in the era of refrigeration and long-distance transport of perishables. At the same time, no matter how interesting locally foraged food is, there's no getting around the fact that spices and rare ingredients from far-off lands will keep landing on menus all over the world.

Hand-in-hand with the emergence of a more globalized culinary landscape, restaurant-goers have changed. Once upon a time, you served only what was on your menu plus a few specials. If someone was a vegetarian I always tried to make something interesting for them, but more often than not, in most restaurants, a plate composed of a few side dishes was all a plant-eater could hope for. Not anymore. Vegetarians, vegans, and gluten-free diners make up more and more of the restaurant-going public. Rather than merely rejecting good food, they want dishes that are as delicious and as meticulously prepared as anything on the meat, fish, poultry, and pasta sides of the menu. For many chefs the effect has been hundreds of new recipes drawing on influences from all over the world to showcase the power of vegetables. For me, it has led to changes in my own diet. Though I'm not a vegetarian, I've always consumed a lot of vegetables; it's just how I grew up. But the new emphasis on bringing convenience to strict vegetarian meals makes it easier for me to eat a diet rich in vegetables but no less delicious and, no doubt, more healthful. Only those chefs who adapt to the new needs of their customers will have a better chance of sustaining in the business.

Decades ago, most of the restaurants that were recognized as the top of the heap were French, with elegant crystal glassware, thick white linens, and pricey porcelain. They were the definition of fine dining and the kind of restaurant that I aspired to run. They held out the allure of more than a superlative meal. They promised refinement, luxury, and elegance, and although pricey, they delivered an experience worth the money. I was lucky enough to apprentice in some of the great ones. Although there still is and, I hope, always will be a place for such temples of French gastronomy, the nature of their dominance has changed. For starters, although French restaurants still occupy a strong presence on the Michelin three-star list, their reign is not unchallenged. Japanese and American chefs combined outnumber the French. Furthermore, whereas elaborate and costly (both to the chef and to the customer) fine dining was the ultimate goal for many chefs, the brutal facts of the economy meant and continue to mean there is only so much room at the top. But happily, traditional fine dining is no longer the only way to offer recipes at the highest level of the chef's craft, nor is it confined to the food-obsessed major cities.

Although it is true that a few major cities still remain hotbeds of new and exciting food trends, more and more of our smaller cities and towns have developed a local clientele that wants and will pay for food just like what is seen on the global scene but created with local talent. At the same time, one of the most heartening developments in the restaurant landscape has been the birth of smaller, more casual restaurants where chefs who are ready to start to climb the ladder can move into their own businesses without being crushed under the massive investment and, often, the mountain of debt that a full-on big-city fine-dining establishment requires. Now we find informal restaurants with less expensive decor and table settings, lower rents, and, crucially, smaller menus. It's been called the bistronomy movement in France, or the rise of gastropubs, and it features skilled chefs who have put in their dues with master chefs in serious restaurants. Cities such as Nashville, Detroit, and Portland, Maine, can offer truly great dishes at more affordable prices. A number of fine chefs who have worked for me have made this move lately. Many of them are thriving, to the delight of their cities.

With a more enthusiastic and adventuresome clientele that displays a willingness to patronize casual places offering great food, and in the face of an online culture that rapidly disseminates new ideas, opportunities to make your mark in this business exist today that were unheard of when I was a young chef. And from the thousands of smaller restaurants continuing to spring up, it is certain that great fine dining will emerge in more places as well.

LETTERS FROM DANIEL

DO YOU REALLY WANT
TO BE A CHEF?

REFLECTING ON THESE letters inevitably reminds me of when I started out in this business many years ago. I had yet to see an avocado, taste a truffle, or eat my first dollop of caviar, which happened to be a spoonful of beluga over a turbot braised in Champagne sauce. I was just a young teenager when I left our family farm in St. Pierre de Chandieu and went to work at Restaurant Nandron in Lyon.

I very soon got my first taste of truffle.

Chef Nandron had just shot a pheasant, grown autumn plump on overripe grapes and juniper berries. He marinated it in Cognac and Madeira, stuffed it with foie gras and the first black truffles of the season, then roasted it in juniper butter, with cabbage, salsify root, and a chunk of country bacon. Even for a kid raised on the glorious food of the Rhône valley this was a sensual revelation. I knew how to hunt and cook a pheasant country style, but that was simple home cooking and this was real cuisine.

Restaurant Nandron was only ten miles down the road from home, but my little village remained much as it had been in the nineteenth century, with the exception of cars and electricity. Lyon, on the other hand, was very much part of the modern world: huge, busy, full of cosmopolitan people with sophisticated tastes. It was a far cry from the Boulud farm, where finding a snake in the barn provided enough excitement for a week's worth of conversation. It was not part of my family's culture to go out to eat at a restaurant. But I loved restaurant work from the moment I tied on a crisp blue apron (only the chefs wore white). It didn't take me long to decide three things: I knew I loved to cook, I knew I wanted to learn from the masters, and I knew that a chef was the only thing I wanted to be.

It was probably a stroke of luck that I didn't know much more. In the beginning, I didn't have a clue how much it would take to go from a lowly worker in a French restaurant to creating a restaurant of my own in New York City; I now know that much more is required than simply knowing how to cook or taking a selfie with a world-famous chef.

People often make that mistake: they confuse skill in the kitchen or social-media savvy with being able to run their own restaurant. I've had some wonderful people work for me who can cook damn well. They have the talent. They've learned from the best. And yet I know that they will fulfill their talents best by maintaining a strong position as a chef for someone else rather than dealing with the hassles of business ownership.

To be a chef, you need to know more than the basics of cooking—from savory to sweet, curing to baking, the almost mystical art of sauces, seasoning, spicing, texture, and taste. Add to that an up-to-date knowledge of or at least acquaintance with the evolving styles of the important contemporary chefs all over the world. Yet this is only the beginning. How to work with people, how to manage them in the cramped quarters and fiery heat of the kitchen, how to practice self-discipline and bring it out in others, where to find the best ingredients (and how to squeeze every penny out of them), how to move around the dining room and be genuinely interested in every customer, how to fulfill the constantly changing food fantasies of a demanding public— these are skills that have nothing to do with shaking the pan but everything to do with whether or not you have what it takes to be a successful chef.

This lengthy list is not meant to discourage you. What I really want is to lay out before you some things you need to consider now, as you begin your career. And as far as I'm concerned, being a chef is a wonderful career. In these letters I will share with you lessons I have learned in the hope that they will help you figure out if this is really the life you want. Of one thing I am sure: the only way you are going to make the grade is if being a chef is indeed what you want most to be.

First, do not be in a hurry. Even if things fall into place perfectly, it will take you at least ten years before you can truly call yourself a chef. No great chef ever became a star without paying his or her dues—"earning their badge," so to speak. It takes time to move up the ladder in a professional kitchen. Learn all you can at every rung; treat each of them as an opportunity to improve your craft that you will never have again as you take on more responsibilities. You will need those years to acquire the culinary craft and absorb the people skills that are required of a chef.

So then the question becomes, how am I going to spend those beginning years? And I would answer that you should begin by finding a mentor in the town you are most familiar with that has very good chefs. After that, travel the world or your country, working as you go, experiencing what is becoming an increasingly globally influenced cuisine. This is a luxury that I did not fully have in my early years, though I did tour most regions of France. Basically, spend a half dozen years or more working for the very best chefs you can find. Bear in mind, traveling is not for everyone, and I know young chefs who have never traveled but are damn good. You will gain a lot more from making salad in the kitchen of a great restaurant than you will from attempting lobster Thermidor in an average joint.

If you are at school in America, you will be what we call a *stagiaire* (or intern), and you may be paid minimum wage. I know that sounds like not much, but in the old days we often worked for no money. There's a lot of competition to get into the best kitchens, and doing so may require that you do whatever it takes to get your foot in the door. Furthermore, once you have that kind of head start on your résumé, you will only advance by working harder and longer than the rest of the kitchen crew so that you are noticed by your chef. If you do this, you will have taken a tremendous first step, because that chef more than likely will give you a full-time position and one day provide a connection to a new job and more education in another restaurant with another talented chef.

I was very fortunate to begin my career in Lyon at a time when France was at the forefront of a culinary revolution. I went from one great restaurant to another, learned as much as I could, and was given more and more responsibility. I learned cooking. I observed a lot about what went into the front and back of the house. And I also learned something about luck.

In those years, when I worked in the kitchens of Roger Vergé, Michel Guérard, and Georges Blanc—at three of the top restaurants in France—I realized that these chefs were never merely lucky. They made their luck by working very hard, honing their skills, and developing their art.

When you go to work in the kitchen of a great chef, chances are you'll learn as much or more from the sous chefs around you and from your fellow cooks in training. The best places attract the best people. You'll learn from them, compete with them, challenge them. Over the years in my kitchens in New York, besides the American cooks and chefs, we have had cooks from all over the world. Every one of them knows something different about cooking, and the exchange is inspiring.

So, with the global nature of modern French kitchens, a chef's education is not as straight a path as the one I took when I left my first job at Nandron after two years and drove sixty miles north to Georges Blanc. A young chef today can make part of the world tour that I mentioned earlier simply by working in the right kitchens in the wide range of cuisines available in most cosmopolitan areas.

After you spend enough years going from kitchen to kitchen, it is time to put down some roots in one place and move up through the ranks. This is when you will take the steps that will make you a true chef. Although you may arrive with a beautiful résumé from some famous restaurants and think you are pretty hot stuff, take my word for it, you are not. Even if you are, it does not mean that much to your chef. He or she is interested only in what is needed in the kitchen, and your goal is to be an asset to their team—not a judge of their place.

Building your ego is not part of the game. This may be hard to swallow after having worked so hard for so long, but there is only room for one ego in a kitchen when the crush of service is on. Do not take it personally. Respect the chef and always give more than expected. Become a key part of the team. This will deepen your technique, your knowledge, and your relationships. It is a critical chapter in your development as a chef. This is when you move from being someone who can cook very well to one who instinctively does it right every time. Your goal must be perfection.

I'm always amazed by the humble artistry of a pizza chef, spinning the dough, tossing it in the air, stretching it into a neat circle. Always perfect. I love it. I wish I knew how to do that. Yet I also know that to be in the same league I would have to spend at least a year at it. It is the same in a restaurant kitchen. You cannot be master of anything unless you work at it for a good long while and really understand it. It has to become second nature to you, and that's why it's good to take time to master every station in a kitchen.

I remember chefs at the restaurants where I apprenticed who had been doing the same thing for ten years and were perfect at it. For any number of reasons, this career path is no longer very common. Perhaps it is the always-online, 24/7, accelerated pace of our lives, the ambition to be famous right away, or the rapidly changing trends in food—whatever the reason, we all work in a charged atmosphere of speed, high expectations, and high ambitions. No one puts in all the time that apprentices once did. You will feel tremendous pressure to move forward as your peers advance. To develop skills the old, slow way is not always practical; still, we can expect perfection in some things and a high degree of competence in others.

I used to give the example of André Soltner, the legendary chef and owner of Lutèce, who—in lieu of reading a résumé—would ask prospective young cooks to make an omelet. Today, I often ask for a simple soup or even an interesting salad with a perfectly balanced vinaigrette. Like the omelet, the whole process takes mere minutes and comprises several critical steps, and in observing them you can instantly assess the level of skill and confidence of any candidate.

You may never be called upon to make an omelet in a fine-dining restaurant, but you will need to strive for the same high level of precision in every aspect of your craft. Spending six months to a year at each station in a restaurant seems just about enough if you practice, keep improving, and keep challenging yourself to make it perfect. The more you look at cooking, the more you realize it is always an unfinished education. There is truly no limit to how much you can learn, especially today, with a global chef community.

Mine is not the only path you can take. Cooking schools produce thousands of graduates each year, but it's important to remember that they've never had to present the bill to a customer or be challenged by food critics for what they made in class, so while many of them have learned a lot, not every one of them will be able to handle the pressures of running a business. Many go to work at hotels, clubs, cruise ships, resorts—all good opportunities—but in a restaurant, the pressures to maintain excellence are higher. I mean, every chef with a reputation must be a great cook first, then be very well organized, have good management skills, understand marketing, have good taste, and know how to control costs. These are skills that you need in a gastronomic restaurant or casual bistro alike. By absorbing everything, you can learn the business. Or you can opt to work in some-one's restaurant for the long haul. Becoming a sous chef to a great chef is an honorable achievement. There is the quiet satisfaction of doing the job of a sous well, and being the most supportive behind-the-scenes chef has its rewards. It can be a fulfilling life.

If you are an entrepreneur, however, there is no limit to how far you can go with your ambition. It takes sacrifice. It will require an understanding that you will work very long hours and not have much of a personal life, but if it is your passion, as it is mine, you do not have much of a choice. You are going to have to do it, so you might as well aim to do it right.

Of course, there are only so many top restaurants that even great cities such as New York, San Francisco, or Los

Angeles can support. Does this mean that you have to make it there? Not anymore. You can be a chef in a smaller city, in such places as Cincinnati or Louisville or Philadelphia, or even in the countryside. Look at Gavin Kaysen in Minneapolis, Minnesota. Gavin was a loyal asset in my restaurants who, as an alumnus, became a friend. Now he's a partner to me in many endeavors, but especially in the foundation Ment'or, which provides grants to train future generations of chefs (www.mentorbkb.org). This is the evolution of chefs in America today: just like Gavin, through dedication and mentorship, younger chefs are able to partner with others and meet the growing demands of a local clientele for better cuisine in small cities. Gavin is helping to expand a culinary identity in Minneapolis. And most important, his cuisine is delicious and soulful, and his restaurant offers warm and knowledgeable service in a cool and cozy atmosphere. America craves those kinds of restaurants, so the opportunities are there. The choice is yours, but the competition is fierce, and you need to know your clientele. The hardest challenge for millennial chefs is to earn loyalty from millennial customers as they search for the latest trends. Being trendy is fantastic, but you need to stay the course. Being successful means outlasting the trend: staying current while maintaining a certain respect for the past; regarding the future in terms of evolution, not revolution.

MENTORS

You will not take the same path that I took, but nonetheless you will proceed from one job to the next as you develop your career. Where do you start? At this stage of the game, no doubt you have some friends who have gone on to good kitchens, or one of your teachers in culinary school noted your raw talent, or maybe you have some family connections. Whatever the case, if you have been studying to be a chef for a few years, you probably know somebody somewhere. My advice is to try them first. It is a big world out there, but it's a small community of chefs; your goal in starting out is to get your foot in the door with a good one. Not one of the great ones necessarily, but someone who knows how to cook very well and, just as important, knows how to run a kitchen that maintains a reputation year in and year out. Be careful of the trendy place where the scene is more important than the food. Look for a place where you can feel genuine soul—in the chef, in the staff, and in the experience they offer.

That first place where you work is an important step for you, because once you are connected within the chef family, your second job will be a whole lot easier to find than the first. At some point you will be able to go to your chef and say that you want to move on, and if you have done a good job and there is no room to advance in his or her kitchen, you can pretty much count on them picking up the phone and making a call for you. Nandron was only too happy to call Georges Blanc for me when that day came. Or maybe the sous chef for whom you worked has moved on and you call him, or maybe a friend of his sends out a call for help. Like most businesses, especially at the top, the restaurant business is one of connections, and you make connections quite obviously by meeting and working with the right people.

What I am talking about here is what people in every walk of life call building your résumé combined with serious networking. I have never hired anybody on the basis of a résumé alone. Ideally they come with a very strong recommendation from their last chef.

So lesson number one: always leave on a good note. If you sign on with somebody whom you look to as a mentor, it is important to make the commitment to stay for two years or so, largely because in the beginning, I promise, you will not be up to speed in the kitchen. By that I mean your skills, knowledge, and palate are still very much works-in-progress. Simply by taking you on, any chef is making an investment in you. You need to stay long enough to pay back that investment—so hopping from one place to the next is the surest way to burn bridges. And in the small world of good restaurants, one burnt bridge can often damage your career. One of the best ways to pay respect to your chef is to find your replacement; as a young cook, you will know many other young cooks. Any chef will remember this gesture. Doing the job well, always being prepared, accepting every task as a challenge, and signing off with integrity are the best things you can do for your résumé and career.

Of course, you may not know anybody at the top, but if you have any connection at all, use it. Take the time to search for an introduction to a good kitchen. Usually people are ready to take a chance on someone young and full of enthusiasm. You might not get paid very much for it. You might have to start at the bottom. In the past, most fine-dining restaurants would offer a low-paying position as a *stagiaire*, or paid intern. It was a great way to prove yourself and learn while having less responsibility than the full-waged cooks. Many people have done stages with me, and like me, most chefs believed an intern's compensation is learning from the organization and making important contacts. Today, these programs are still common in Europe. They remain less common in the United States, and they are no less important for young cooks.

I can guarantee that cooking today is much more fun, honorable, and rewarding for everyone in the business than when I started. I was barely a teenager when I started at Nandron. It was a very good restaurant (two stars), and I was at the bottom of the heap. I learned how to peel every vegetable, filet every fish, and pluck every game bird in the Lyon markets. I got my knife skills together. I learned the importance of MEP—*mise en place*—the term for the art of creating your recipe in "kit" form, that is, broken down into preproduced elements so that you are ready before the crush of service, at which point all you have to do is cook, finish, and assemble it, rapidly.

As low man on the team, my job was to go to the market in Lyon first thing in the morning to pick up supplies. Guess who else was there? The legendary chefs of Lyon and its environs who were in the vanguard of new French cooking: the Troisgros brothers, Paul Bocuse, Georges Blanc, and Alain Chapel. For a chef, being in Lyon in those days was like being a musician in Liverpool when the Beatles were getting together. These were the guys who were changing the food world. They were at the market early to make sure they got the very best ingredients before anybody else had a chance to buy them. There were beautiful vegetables from the farms of the Rhône and wild herbs and cheeses from the mountains of eastern France and glistening fish fresh from the Mediterranean and the Atlantic.

Working long hours—which every young chef had to do—and then getting up super early to be at the market is tough: definitely not the most sought-after job. But taking on the tough jobs—from scouring pots and cleaning vegetables to showing up before dawn rubbing the sleep from your eyes—is the mark of someone who will pay their dues to learn *everything* about the job of being a chef. Early mornings in the market had their rewards: I had the chance to rub elbows with the greats. This does not mean that I was able or even tried to get a job with them, but I got to see how great chefs act and think and handle ingredients, and that was invaluable. Once the trip to the market was done, I would sit down at one of the local *bouchons* and have a bowl of tripe with them. They would open a bottle of Beaujolais (but I stuck with lemonade). The stories, the pungent rough language, the camaraderie made me feel on top of the world. Of course, they would rag me pretty hard in the way that old pros like to tease a young kid. But I ate it up. I was just so happy to be in their company.

After three years of apprenticeship at Nandron, I figured I had learned about all I was going to learn. Nandron understood that, and I was off to my next mentor: Georges Blanc. It was a good fit for me, because like me, Blanc came from a family that had a tradition of serving what was known as the grandmother cuisine of the area. He was interested in refining this traditional food into haute cuisine and shooting for three Michelin stars. His family-style cuisine had become world famous at his mother's auberge, La Mère Blanc, a wonderful two-star restaurant near the old wine route between Burgundy and Lyon. But Blanc elevated that country food to an art. Something as simple as Blanc's frog's legs, which you could get anywhere, were the best frog's legs you could ever hope to have: perfectly crisp, seasoned, moist, and finely balanced between the full aromas of garlic, shallots, and the herbal accents of parsley and chervil.

As I look at the modern dining landscape and see first the advent of comfort food and then the reinvention of that food on contemporary American menus, I recognize a process that I first experienced working with Georges Blanc. My strong advice to you, which I learned from a three-star Michelin chef, is "Remember your grandmother's food!" That is shorthand for saying remember the foods that connect you to your region, your family, and your culture, and celebrate your heritage. If I had to pick one dish that seemed to conjure up this idea for Blanc, it would be *crêpes vonnassiennes:* crispy, moist pancakes made from a batter incorporating mashed potatoes—and soft with a buttery perfume. The recipe actually came from his grandmother, who used leftover mashed potatoes for the batter. I'm sure he grew up making and eating them, and he still serves them today. It is like Proust and his madeleine: once you start thinking of a favorite dish from your childhood, it summons up a whole world. When you are a chef, you are going to want to honor your past by transforming food memories into offerings that belong in a great restaurant, so that they are new and current yet fundamentally classic.

When you work with a great chef, your job is not to be creative but rather to interpret the creativity of the chef for whom you are working. The chef has an idea for a dish that comes from a deep understanding of cooking and ingredients. If you can help interpret his ideas, his inspiration, and his techniques consistently, you will enrich your foundation as a chef.

For example, I used to work with Blanc to develop new dishes. When he had an idea for a new dish he would explain the concept and basics to me, and I would make a test and do the *mise en place*. He would taste and approve it, or, if not, would guide me as to how to make it better. This was true whether the dish was as simple as a sorbet or as inspired and complex as a *poularde de bresse* stuffed with crayfish, chicken liver, foie gras, porcini, and truffle. During the experimentation phase of any dish, there is constant communication between the chef and the cook, who work together to gradually bring the dish into harmony with the chef's vision. Getting it right was a tremendous satisfaction. It's the same process today with my team of chefs and their sous chefs.

Blanc and Nandron were chefs in the Burgundian and Lyonnais traditions: founded on broad flavors as seductive as Burgundy wine (which was used in many of the recipes). Blanc was an innovator, but his tastes always had an authentic link to the classically pungent flavors of the region. My next mentor was Roger Vergé at Le Moulin de Mougins on the French Riviera. In the same way that my job with Blanc resulted from a phone call from Nandron, another phone call, this time from Blanc, landed me with Vergé. The year was 1974.

Vergé was from Allier, near the center of France. He had traveled the world and finally settled in the south of France, where he embraced the sunny, light cuisine of Provence—as bright as a Van Gogh sunflower. His was probably the most fashionable and stylish restaurant in the world during the mid-1970s. It was a Mecca for the next generation of talented young chefs. Alain Ducasse worked there before he went on to Michelin superstardom. David Bouley, Hubert Keller, Jacques Chibois, Francis Mallmann, Emeril Lagasse, and George Mendes all worked there too, and went on to great success in their own restaurant ventures. As they did for me, the years spent learning from Vergé served those chefs well.

Le Moulin de Mougins was my first three-star restaurant (Blanc was still a two when I was there) and a whole new level of the game. Working in a stable of such thoroughbreds made each of us better. We learned the same lesson that you could learn at any great restaurant with the same ambition: although everything is based on the skill and reputation of the chef at the top, cooking is a team sport.

In the beginning, when you are cooking another person's cuisine, it is discipline, not your creativity, that is the most important quality. Expressing what the chef wants and doing so with his or her team requires it. This is not to say that your ultimate goal is to be a clone of your mentor. Just as there was only one Roger Vergé, there is only one you. The young chef who strives to learn everything a mentor can teach will be more ready someday to express his or her own creativity when the time comes. I have seen this happen time and again with young chefs who made the transition to master in their own right. For example, Corey Lee, whose San Francisco restaurant Benu has earned three Michelin stars, perfected and refined the cuisine of the French Laundry during his years with Thomas Keller. Once he struck out on his own, his marriage of French technique, California ingredients, affinity for Cantonese cuisine, and Korean background made his inspired food unique and personal. It's clear he learned many things from his years with Keller but at the same time was developing his own style.

What did I learn with Vergé? Better to ask, what didn't I learn? Every one of my cooking skills was honed. I took the beginning steps as a chef de partie, running the garde manger (cold appetizers and soup) station and the braising station. I

can still smell and taste his lamb shoulder Provençale that I
made so many times. It was braised slowly overnight in a casserole sealed with bread dough so that not a waft of aroma or
flavor escaped. It was rich in herbs fresh picked from Vergé's
garden: rosemary, basil, thyme, bay leaf. To this he added
spice accents with star anise, fennel, coriander, and orange
peel, and a mirepoix with garlic, onions, carrots, tomatoes,
mushrooms, turnips, and celery. The braising liquid consisted
of red wine, olive oil, and orange juice, which seemed wild to
me at the time. Fresh pork rind tied into small bundles gave
body and a satiny unctuousness to the stew. What a novel,
powerhouse idea! The result was a sublimely light, heady, and
fragrant stew—a marriage of personal touch and tradition
that made the dish simple yet unforgettable.

In addition to the deep braising of lamb, veal, beef, and
poultry, it was at the braising station where we did the initial
prep for Vergé's sauces, which were the anchor of his cuisine.
Sauces are their own discipline. Everything you know about
flavor and balance is concentrated to the nth degree. What
tastes too strong in the saucepan will play spectacularly on
the plate, and you have to be able to imagine the effect of the
end result just by tasting what's in the pan. I remember a velvety sauce for duck made with the blood of the duck, giblets,
a traditional mirepoix, Provençal herbs, and figs. It was so
complex yet at the same time so focused. For Vergé, to make
a good sauce, one had to consider taste, color, texture, shine,

consistency, and seasoning. Above all, the length and finish on the palate was the ultimate goal.

To this day, I merely have to see the words *sauce au poivre* on a menu to think of Vergé's reinvention of that classic sauce: the sweet and spicy Sauce Mathurini made with cracked exotic pepper, golden raisins, cognac, and extremely full-flavored beef stock. Vergé could move easily from the big tastes of meat and game sauces to a whimsical and delicate Sauce Poivre Rose—a light, creamy emulsion of paprika and sweet Sauternes, brought to a briny finish with Mediterranean rock lobster.

I learned cooking with all my mentors, but just as important, I observed the management side of their cuisine, which is equally valuable to my success as a chef. As you move up through the ranks of a great kitchen, you pick up management by watching the people above you, watching the chef, and understanding his or her responsibility.

You may have all the creativity in the world, but it won't guarantee you success in a restaurant, because if you cannot run a team, you cannot run a restaurant. You must first learn to manage the requirements at every step in the career ladder. In a classic kitchen brigade, commis is the first rung. One of the commis chef's primary tasks is efficiently organizing the prep work, or *mise en place* (MEP). Further up the totem pole you'll graduate to chef de partie, where you'll be in charge of a few cooks. If you do that well, the next step is sous chef, where you could be in charge of even more cooks—as many as ten in an upscale restaurant. However high you ascend, it always starts with self-management.

Management is where the fantasy of being a chef runs into the business end. You go into cooking, no doubt, because you find it pleasurable. But business always comes before pleasure, and today more than ever you have to be concerned with the economic side of restaurant management. Learning that fact as a young chef will be invaluable to you later. The connection to your mentor, the understanding of what he or she does to run a successful business—these are things that you acquire over years.

Apparently I did, because after a few years, when I felt it was time to move on from Vergé, he had a surprise for me. "How would you like to go to Denmark and be sous chef at a restaurant for me, teaching the Danish chef my cuisine?" he asked. "I think it will be a good test for you."

Hello? Denmark? That came out of left field. On the one hand, at twenty-one I still felt very young and inexperienced, yet I had absorbed a lot in my seven years working in the kitchen, including two with Vergé. I had risen to chef de partie. This would be a big jump, though not exactly what I had planned. There were openings at another pair of three-star Michelin restaurants—Troisgros and Chapel—and I felt I had a pretty good shot at either place.

Denmark, though, was a whole new world. It was really my first chance to indulge the chef's fantasy of taking his skills anywhere and making a living while learning a new culture. Our profession is one of the few that affords you this freedom. If you are a lawyer or a doctor or a stockbroker, you will find it difficult to just pull up stakes and start over in a new country. As a chef, however, you take your knives and your passport and you chop onions in any country that will have you.

My year and a half in Denmark was a happy time. I rode my bicycle everywhere. I learned a lot about using spices like caraway seed, cumin, and other dried seeds that play such a large part in traditional Nordic flavors, and about curing fish. (This was well before the appearance of Noma and the resurgence of foraging for lichens, mosses, and seaweed.) I learned independence away from the womb of French cooking. I picked up a good deal about managing people, but after a year and a half, I said, "I've done it. That's it. I've learned a lot, been fairly compensated, and had a great time, but my education is not over." Again it was time to go back to the grind. I wanted to work in another three-star.

I heard from a friend whom I knew through Vergé, Didier Oudill, about an opening at Michel Guérard (see what I mean about friends and connections you make from one kitchen to the next?). I thought about it and decided,

"Hey, I'm still young. I can afford to make (practically) no money and learn from the best." So I made the decision to work my way back up the totem pole and take a big pay cut to do it. In the long run, I figured it would pay off.

Guérard, in Eugénie-les-Bains, was the high priest of lightness and ingredient-driven cuisine. He had taken an unusual route to chefdom: the pastry kitchen. Only after a successful pastry career in Paris did he embrace and advance the emerging style of nouvelle cuisine. Not only that, but when he opened his first restaurant, Le Pot au Feu, it was in a very blue-collar neighborhood. The food was so astonishing that soon this bohemian bistro became the rage of Paris. Guérard learned from his mentor, Jean Delaveyne, an underrated but hugely influential chef who was among the forefathers of nouvelle cuisine.

So my new mentor had his own mentor. And you could trace Delaveyne no doubt back to Escoffier, Curnonsky, Gouffé, and so on, all the way back to the godfather of haute cuisine, Carême. Many musicians, painters, dancers, and actors do the same type of studying along a lineage of style. In any art, to connect with the great chain of masters stretching back through history is both humbling and exhilarating.

Guérard, partly by personality and partly by virtue of his background, was meticulous to the point of obsession over the tiniest details. We made a rabbit casserole that included young turnips (both the root and the delicate greens), sage, savory, garlic sprouts, and *ognoasse*, a sweet spring onion found in the southwest of France. The vegetables and the rabbit cooked together, but in separate stages: their juices were constantly reduced, concentrated, and combined. The same attention to detail characterized the preparation of every part of every recipe according to its requirements, with all steps perfectly marrying into a finished whole.

At the same time, Guérard was almost spiritual about cooking, and in that regard I have always thought of him as the poet of French cuisine. Precision in technique and poetry in approach—at the time I could not think of two better qualities for a chef. He taught me about sensibility, good taste, perfect ingredients, and the mission of the chef to present the true, pristine flavors of each ingredient. Take his Salade Gourmande (in the 1980s, the fine-dining world's most copied salad): a green-bean salad, the haricots as thin as needles, with shaved foie gras poached in duck fat, white asparagus showered with slivers of black truffles, tossed with chervil, chive, and crisp heart of radicchio. Very simple, but if it didn't have the crisp bean, cooked perfectly, the rich foie gras, the most pungent truffle, the freshest asparagus and bitter lettuce, then the result would be pretentious and not very good. Every step had to be precise and perfect. Guérard was very demanding and would not settle for less than your best. If you missed one step in a recipe that called for thirty-five ingredients, he would always know it—and you were dead meat.

With Guérard I arrived at a golden moment, in February, two months before his restaurant was to reopen for the season. Guérard had plans for a shop in Paris at Place de la Madeleine, right next to Hédiard and Fauchon, the world's greatest épiceries. So there were four of us—Guérard, Didier Oudill (executive chef), Jacky Lanusse (chef de cuisine), and me—in this small town in France in the middle of nowhere, and Guérard had enlisted us to work full-time on the creation of new dishes and products for the restaurant and shop.

In this business, rarely does one get to work in the R&D department with such a great chef so closely and so directly in the act of creation. Sometimes when a chef writes a cookbook, a young chef collaborates on testing and refining dishes, so I was not the only one to have this experience, but during this time, Guérard was young and whimsical, at his peak in terms of creativity, and was establishing a solid reputation and following. I felt honored to be a part of it all.

Sometimes Guérard's team would combine his vision with the techniques we had learned working in other places all over France. So what I said about subordinating your creativity to the vision of your chef is still true, but sometimes it can result in being called on to create in your own right. Our collective knowledge made us able to better execute his ideas and his vision.

This is the way of the world, not only in cooking. Work with a master. Learn to think like the master. And one day the master will have the confidence to ask you to move his or her work forward. When this happens, you are on your way to being your own master—or at least, you have taken a first step.

HEAT

———————◆———————

BECOMING A CHEF, like making a good stock, needs unhurried, unpressured time. It takes years to master the basic process of cuisine: heat. Roasting, braising, sautéing, and basting are to my mind the important methods in the foundation of French cuisine. Today, many forms of heat have their uses—steaming, poaching, grilling, broiling, sous vide—but in the classical French kitchen the master of heat is first and foremost one who can roast, braise, and sauté. That's why thick and heavy copper pots play such a big role. They are the best conductors of heat, and to me they will always be the best partner to the chef.

Cuisiner (to cook) literally means to add heat to food. The idea is simple; the variations are infinite. Your range of temperatures is vast—from roughly 130°F/54°C for a slow confit of salmon in oil or sous vide to 900°F/500°C for tandoori lamb. When you understand heat, you "see" food down to its very molecules. You will sense that ingredients have been transformed by heat into something tasty, sensual, and satisfying.

These mystical gifts of sight and sensation are nothing more than the experience gained from making thousands of dishes so that a simple touch or smell will tell you exactly when something is done. Following a recipe by rote will never allow you to achieve this result. Every ingredient is unique and will respond to heat differently. Developing this sixth sense will give you the confidence of precision and help you adapt to any variation in an ingredient. Each must be watched, prodded, and smelled until you sense, because you have cooked the recipe a hundred times before, that it is done. At its core, this process is nothing more than chemistry. The chef's job—to employ heat to transform ingredients—is the closest thing to alchemy I have come across. Mastering such intuition comes from years of work and practice, yet the results, when they are right, feel truly like the work of magic, and they instill a sense of pride in the art of mastering the perfect *cuisson*.

I once made a quail stuffed with foie gras and figs—three ingredients that require different cooking times. I could have roasted everything independently and made a nice dish, but I thought it would be more interesting all cooked together. If I had stuffed the quail and roasted it until the foie gras was done, I might have had perfectly cooked foie gras but a bird with the texture of denim and figs turned to runny mush. Clearly not my goal.

What I needed to do—*before* stuffing—was to pre-sear and halfway cook the slice of foie gras. I also used ripe figs so that warming them would just soften them. To execute this in the kitchen, logic required three steps in heating. Understanding the interplay between heat and ingredients, however, allowed me to achieve a single combined recipe that produced a roasted whole quail split in half with perfectly pink breast meat, glistening foie gras, and velvety soft fig.

Some years later, in preparing one of my quarterly fifteen-course blowouts for the renowned wine expert Bob Parker and his friends, I decided to up the ante and complicate the whole thing. I wanted to do a Ballotine (a boneless rolled and stuffed roast) of Duck, Foie Gras, and Figs. I made a boneless butterflied duck stuffed with spiced figs wrapped in a thin slice of speck ham, and whole fresh foie gras marinated in Sauternes, salt, pepper, and a spice mix of cinnamon, star anise, powdered clove, and grated orange zest.

Once stuffed, the duck was trussed with twine to its original shape. To finish, I had a range of different heat goals. This time I preroasted the foie gras (about one and a half pounds) in its own fat until it was half done. In other words, I didn't need the foie gras to be as precooked as I did in the quail, because by the time the duck was roasted to moist pinkness, it would allow the partially cooked foie gras time to release its fat to infuse the figs, speck, and duck meat. While the duck roasted, it was glazed and basted with a blend of spiced honey, salt, and reduced citrus juice to give it a glistening crust. So I was striving to achieve different levels of doneness while controlling many ingredients, all with differing textures and flavors. Before serving, we presented it as Escoffier might have done: on a silver platter that glittered like the full moon on the ocean, the glistening, glazed *ballotine* in the center surrounded by a ring of endive caramelized in orange glaze. Slicing the roast released a puff of sweet, spicy aroma. On the plate you had a golden-brown skin as an outer ring and rosy, succulent duck meat below with a firm and fatty foie gras and a sweet and salty boudin of fruit and ham in the center. A spectacular dish—and one that Bob Parker raved about for years. It is the challenge of transforming a dish like this that excited me.

The fundamental method of transforming food through heat is, to my mind, roasting. If the hearth is the heart of the home, the rotisserie station is the heart of the restaurant. Roasting is not a fast process. When you roast, you cannot walk away from it the way you can leave a stock while it simmers, a dish while it braises, or sous vide in a water bath. You must stay connected to the food when you roast. You need to touch, smell, and baste every so often. You need to add flavors—vegetables, butter or other fat, and aromatics—at certain times so that they are finished just when the roast is finished. This keeps you focused on the line. In a busy restaurant it is a constant juggle, managing various types of meat, their cuissons, and their methods of roasting. It's a true test of a great cook to master all this with perfect seasoning and doneness.

On the other hand, when I'm at home, a great roast—say, a chicken—becomes the centerpiece of the day, in both the cooking and the eating. The first consideration is the chicken. You need a good, organic bird. Clean it well, pat it dry, truss it, and let it air dry in the fridge overnight so the skin is no longer wet. Season it inside with salt and pepper, and add garlic, shallots, parsley, and thyme to the cavity. When you're ready to cook it, season the outside with salt and pepper, and rub the skin with soft butter. Set the chicken in a pan that is generously larger than the bird. Place the pan in a 425°F oven and roast for half the allotted cooking time (which depends on the size of the chicken, of course), basting with first-quality butter all the while. Halfway through the cooking process, I throw in a pound of small German butterball potatoes, a pound of cipollini onions, and a whole head of peeled garlic cloves. Then a small bundle of fresh thyme and parsley stems, and some half-inch cubes of bacon or pancetta. Ten minutes later, add a pound of porcini or other meaty mushrooms, and season with salt and pepper. I lower the heat to 325°F, allowing the chicken to release more fat for the vegetables and finish to a golden-brown juiciness. When the chicken is done, let it rest for 15 minutes, and finish cooking the vegetables if they need it. Finally, toss in some parsley leaves. I have been roasting this way at home since I was a teenager, and I have yet to meet the high-tech setup that can do it better.

In the restaurant, the rôtisseur (cook in charge of roasted items) might repeat this process for twenty chickens in a day, yet he or she must give the same care and attention to a half dozen things at once—from duck to chicken to squab to venison. Each has a different process and cycle of preparation. A good rôtisseur must have an intuitive connection to each type of meat.

With only the outside of the meat to look at, you must be able to imagine—very vividly—the transformation of juice, the firming of flesh, and the concentration of flavor that are going on deep inside. And then you must be able to think from there to the plate.

At the same time, you have to deal with the question of seasoning, an essential element in transforming merely hot meat into a precious moment of savory, succulent gastronomy.

Each cut of animal has its own demands. Often you season before you roast, so that as the outer layer of meat caramelizes in the gentle searing of its initial exposure to heat, the seasoning pulls and concentrates flavor to the surface while gently penetrating the flesh. You may also season during the roasting process. If it is a whole fowl or fish, then you season the cavity as well so the seasoning permeates the flesh from the inside. Finally, after carving or slicing the roast, you lightly season the center cut again so that the first thing your taste buds react to is seasoning, opening up your palate.

Resting is nearly as important as roasting. You cannot hurry roasting, nor can you be in a rush to serve the roast. Meat must rest after roasting to maintain juiciness, and it is a cardinal rule of cuisine that holding the juices in the meat is the hallmark of properly roasted and served meat. How long should it rest? It depends on the meat. A thick cut of beef might rest for half an hour or more, allowing the juices to be reabsorbed into the flesh (although in the delicious, juicy, *churrascaria* style, the meat is sliced fresh from the fire). Venison, a different story, is not very fatty—it does not have space in its fibers to absorb and hold moisture. If you leave it to rest for too long, the juices will evacuate the meat, and you will be left with a bland, uninteresting taste. My chestnut-crusted loin of venison is served very pink, because overcooked venison is unsalvageably tough and dry. I rest it for just a few minutes then slice it so that the juice and blood pearl on top of the slice. Then I add some sea salt and pepper, and it is perfect.

It takes a very good cook to be a rôtisseur. As I mentioned before, all cooks want to work on the line—they think they are going to earn more respect if they are flipping pans. But roasting teaches you an understanding of main ingredients (meat, fowl, fish) that is deeper and that will make you a better chef on the line. Of course these days, the old-fashioned way of roasting and feeling the cuisson under your fingers is supported by use of a tester (a small needle), which helps you gauge the internal temperature for doneness. You insert the tool into the roast and then place it below your lips to judge the temperature. For a big roast use a probe thermometer. If your prep is all sous vide, then you don't have to be too much of an expert rôtisseur to accomplish the job.

Next in importance to roasting is braising. Quite literally, *to braise* means to cook on a *braisier*—that is, over embers. Practically speaking, it involves cooking food that is barely immersed in liquid to slowly draw out the fat and juice from meats as well as the juices and flavors from herbs and vegetables. It is all about slow cooking and basting often. The braising pot is the cook's magic cauldron where flavors swirl, combine, concentrate, transform.

Braising—a rustic form of cooking used in nearly every cuisine—is not without art or the demand of the chef's constant attention, though less so than with roasting. One thing it is not is simply putting some liquid and some meat in a pot, covering it, and letting it bubble away for a few hours. Braising is not stewing, because it is only half immersed in liquid. It is sort of half stewing and half wet roasting. That is why basting is important. As the flavors in the braising liquid concentrate, you keep basting, building up a glacé on the meat that is both concentrated and flavorful. At the same time, you are reducing the liquid—not only the liquid that you start braising with, but also the juices extracted by heat from the vegetables and meat. The reducing and glazing return these flavors to the meat.

If you end up with a lot of braising liquid, you have not concentrated the flavors enough. A properly braised piece of meat or fowl or fish has just enough liquid for that serving and no more. Do not shortchange your recipe. Give back to the plate every iota of flavor that the ingredients started with.

To me, braising is the deep soul of French cooking. When I think of the classic French braises, it takes me on a culinary tour of France—for example, a lamb shank. If I think of Provence, I think of braising the lamb in garlic, herbs, orange zest, olives, tomatoes, and a floral white wine. For the same piece of lamb in Burgundy, I taste a braising liquid of red wine, roasted onions, celery root, *lard de campagne,* wild mushrooms. Lamb shank in the southwest is going to be braised with a more Spanish and mountain feel—lots of onions, peppers with some heat to them, tomatoes. At the other corner of France, it will be Alsatian Baeckeoffe style— lamb shoulder braised with pork shoulder, Riesling, onions, and potatoes.

Braising reveals the beauty and depth—both historical and cultural—of French cooking. Not only does gastronomic cooking embrace all these regions, refining their traditions, but it also draws on bistro cooking and *cuisine bourgeoise* (think of the normal Sunday meal for a French family). In all French cuisine, braising is a major element. I'm also a big fan of every country's tradition of braising and wrote a book on the topic, *Braise: A Journey Through International Cuisine.*

Okay, I know you want to get to the line, so let's do it. The main activity on the meat and fish lines is sautéing. The textbook definition of *sautéing* is to cook something in a little bit of fat at high heat. But in this simple definition there is a whole range of variations.

Call me old-school but I still think copper is best. Aluminum is fine for boiling and baking but not for pan roasting. Copper, though, can get very hot, and you can smoothly control every temperature. When we make a chicken *jus* in a copper roasting pan, we heat the pan until it is super hot before we put the bones in to roast, which lets us begin with a good sear and caramelization. Cast iron is also a great heat carrier: like copper, it gets very hot and distributes heat evenly. It is very good for coloring bones and meat before you deglaze. A word about meat caramelization: you want it *brown,* not a light tan. The surface of well-seared meat develops sweetness and nuttiness and a crust with flavor and texture elements without which meat can be bland and uninteresting.

In the modern kitchen we use induction stoves that employ magnetic resonance; cast iron works very well with this high-tech method. For pan roasting, I like a black steel pan well-seasoned from the constant use of the same application (just like the Chinese do with their woks). Stainless-steel pans are ubiquitous because they are easy to cook with and maintain, but certain jobs require other materials. Ideally you have the whole range in your kitchen.

With root vegetables I like to let the flavor develop slowly and concentrate before I caramelize the outside. Many cooks will blanch their vegetables, then throw them into a hot pan with oil or butter. I feel that one preserves pristine flavor more fully when you put the vegetables in a pan, add a little bit of butter, some herbs and aromatics, and slowly heat them, rolling them over and over in the butter (adding a few drops of water as needed). At this gentle heat, they will be slightly steamed in their own moisture; *sweating* and *glazing* are terms we often use for this process. In a simple carrot preparation, I start with a little butter (or olive oil) and chicken stock and fresh sage, then simmer until they are firm but getting tender. By this time, they have reabsorbed all their juices and released their sugars, which then glaze up beautifully. Covering the pan (for the initial wet cooking) with a lid or parchment paper aids this process enormously, allowing evaporation but at a rate that is, say, 20 percent, as opposed to 100 percent for an uncovered pan.

We also *arroser*—that is, baste with butter. Here, for example, a fish filet is cooked in a hot pan. You keep spooning butter over the fish so that while it cooks and roasts on the bottom, hot butter seeps in and slowly cooks the flesh on top. The butter has to be hot, foamy, seasoned, and plentiful enough to really shower the fish. Be careful, though, that you don't use butter as a cure-all to mask less-than-perfect technique.

These methods of heating have changed very little since Roze de Chantoiseau opened the first modern restaurant in Paris in 1766. Actually they've changed very little since the days of Charlemagne, but in the last twenty years restaurants everywhere have adopted the nearly fail-proof method known as sous vide. Once an expensive luxury, it is now at least somewhat familiar to any serious chef. By sealing food in an air-tight bag and immersing it in a low-temperature water bath, almost any chef can create juicy, deeply flavored meats and vegetables. Sometimes sous vide is an intermediate cooking step. For example, a beautiful strip steak can be cooked sous vide to a perfect medium-rareness all the way through, but then you need to finish it over high heat to create the all-important crust that is the hallmark of a good steak. At other times, however—for example, with chicken—you seal the meat in a bag with a bit of fat, and some herbs, spices, and other seasonings, and you will have succulent white meat . . . *every time!* But remember, sous vide uses a machine and is based on technology, not cooking. Playing with it may give you great, consistent results, but it doesn't give you the knowledge, the instinct, and the pleasure of cooking in the traditional methods.

In so much of what we have touched on in this letter—whether it is extracting and reabsorbing juice in roasting, or braising and reducing, or sautéing then caramelizing—you are working the moisture in the food, and then concentrating it and reintegrating it back into the ingredient. Heat, concentrate, reintegrate. No matter how you apply heat, this is the transformational aspect of cuisine. How good your food is depends on how well you control this force of nature.

FLAVOR

―――――◆―――――

FLAVOR, THE INTERPLAY of taste and aroma, is very personal. Developing your sense of flavor is one of the most important aspects of becoming a chef. True, there are people who have fantastic palates who are not chefs. There are no chefs, however—or at least none of any note—who do not have a highly developed sense of flavor. That sense will vary from chef to chef. Peppery, smoky, salty, raw, cooked, sweet, tangy, spicy, etc.—flavors can come from a range of a single ingredient to many ingredients. An ingredient's applications, combinations, and transformations create a unique taste and texture, the two of which together impart flavor. One may express undercurrents of brininess, another may accent the herbal style of a region of mountain grasses and wildflowers, another the hot and spicy kick given to tamer ingredients by the endless variety of chilies. These accents, part personal and part cultural, make for the diversity and delightful surprises in restaurant cuisine.

Flavor is always present, but its composition is not always perceptible. When you listen to a symphony, you may hear the trumpets ring out, but unless you are a trained musician you probably will not be able to distinguish between the violas and cellos, for example. Nonetheless, they are there and they are important. Remove one or the other and most of us may not be able to tell what exactly is missing, but we will know that the sound is somehow unbalanced, less than full.

It is the same with flavor. In some recipes there is a dominating overall flavor that may mask or at least mute the underlying levels of flavor. In a pâté of guinea hen and smoked pork belly, for example, the pleasantly gamey flavor of cured and smoky pork will rise over the hen, foie gras, and spices. Only after you bite and chew and breathe through your nose does the palate "round out" and the full flavor come through: a delicious mélange of liver, mushroom, chestnut, sweet onion, and garlic, the clarity of allspice and clove, the novel fragrance of pink peppercorn. All these are nearly as important as the delicate piece of fowl that supports everything.

One thing that influences flavor but has nothing to do with taste buds is texture. With many dishes, your mouth seeks out texture first before it "decides" to experience taste. That is one of the fascinating things about taste: you prepare yourself mentally beforehand. Texture is a critical messenger in alerting you to what is coming. The satiny smoothness then brittleness of chocolate; the chewy, sinewy unctuousness of a well-marbled porterhouse steak; the crackle of a crispy rice-flour crust on shrimp tempura—all these elements set up the actual palate experience that follows. Without texture, without touching and feeling, the most exquisite flavors are reduced to boring uniformity. Creating and controlling texture is yet another reason for the importance of mastering heat when you roast, sauté, braise, grill, or sous vide. With control of heat, you can determine the way your tongue first experiences the texture of the food you are preparing.

I should also mention something that often precedes texture: aroma. Sit in a dining room when the waiters shave a bulbous white truffle over a steaming risotto: the funky, almost sexy, aroma will reach you, quite powerfully, from fifty feet away. Up close it is as if you are wrapped in a truffle aura, a distillation of all the aromas of an autumn hillside in Alba—fermented wild berries, decaying oak leaves, musk of wild boar, smoky pine balsam.

Or to take a less rarefied (and less costly) example, think about a soup. What do you do when a hot bowl of soup is put in front of you? A chef will always "grab steam," directing the wafts of vapor coming off, say, a prawn broth with accents of lemongrass, lime, and holy basil. You are wrapped up in a haze of anticipation and appetite even before anything hits your tongue.

So, flavor is not a static thing. There is no simple, official "Flavor of Pike Quenelles in Nantua Sauce" or "Flavor of Roasted Grouse in a Foamy Brown Butter with Juniper, Sage, and Orange Peel." There is not even a simple "Flavor of Carrot." Throw some almond shells in the garden bed— as Dan Barber did—and you will have carrots that carry a pleasing echo of almond. Harvest a certain strain of young carrot from mineral-rich topsoil, and you will add sweetness from the first crunchy bite. Furthermore, you need to think of flavor the way you experience a performance. Just as there is a beginning, middle, and end to a play, there is a similar narrative to tasting. Usually flavor starts with aroma, then moves to texture, then to the actual experience on the tongue, and finally, as you chew, swallow, and breathe out, there is another waft of aroma that rises from your palate into your nostrils.

As a chef, you must be in control of all these elements and determine how strong and long-lasting each of them will be. For example, adding rosemary to the olive oil–crisped skin of a freshly caught sea bass will wake up your palate right away, first from the flavoring on the outside, which will fade as the deeper yet subtle, pristine flavor of the bass comes through.

Yet I might want to lengthen that herbal flavor on the palate, as I do with velvety pea soup topped with smooth rosemary-infused cream. Here the richness of the cream "spreads out" the pungent herb and extends the flavor so that the relatively mild sweet pea picks up dimension and character. Any fat in food, light or rich, will expand and carry the flavor profile.

Once you understand that there are many facets to the flavor of each ingredient, you may overcome a common (usually fatal) tendency to achieve more flavor by complicating the recipe. Believe me, less is more when it comes to flavor. Consider the endless possibilities in the final product in winemaking. Although a great wine may combine a number of varieties in its "recipe," wine still has only one major ingredient: the grape. But through the winemaker's labors, it expresses an infinite series of variations in the complex preparation of the vineyard, the soil, and the fermentation to make every vintage a new wine, a new taste in nuance.

Similarly, for each ingredient included in a recipe, you must have an intimate knowledge of its flavor profile. For example, we make a carrot coulis by sweating, steaming, or slow-baking very fresh, crisp carrots to concentrate their sweet flavor. Then we make a juice of raw carrots to preserve a pristine, fresh flavor. We blend the two and may add a pinch of acidity to liven up the mix—such as lime, which accents the fresh-from-the-garden flavors of the carrot. Very simple. Just one extra clean but sharp ingredient—lime—affects a happy marriage of the cooked and uncooked flavors, of sweet and tart. Of course, this is just a simple base; spices and seasoning complete the process.

Same case with fruit. You might want to expand flavors from one ingredient, such as apricots, and make an apricot-custard tart with vanilla-poached apricot. We top the tart with fresh apricot coulis and serve it with a roasted-apricot and almond ice cream. Voila! Different textures and flavors of the apricot in one dish. Think of the cubist paintings of Picasso or Braque, which simultaneously present different aspects of the same form from different angles to compose a still-life portrait or landscape with depth and artistic taste—just like cooking. We are coaxing layers of flavor and surprises from one ingredient.

In considering specific flavors, I start with salt, the most fundamental of seasonings. As I explained, you may salt before you cook, while you cook, and as you plate. In each instance the salt does something a little different. Added at the beginning, it helps fix the tastes, such as when making a simple soup; if you forget the salt it is very difficult to obtain a good taste. To concentrate the flavors during roasting, salt helps to form a better seasoning, which in part depends on the thickeners used. Then, after the meat is rested and sliced, a sprinkling of coarse salt on top will help pull the deep flavors out of the meat while leaving a brittle *fleur de sel* texture that is even more concentrated.

A good chef's primary concern for a successful dish, you will have noticed by now, starts with the perfect touch of salt to slowly adjust the balance of flavor. For quite a while most chefs banned salt and pepper from the dining table, the implication being that the dish came from the kitchen perfectly seasoned. I'm in total agreement, but in fact all of us have different thresholds of flavor, and what is undersalted to me might be just right for you. So, if asked to, we offer the finest crystals of natural sea salt at the table so that diners can make a personal adjustment. Whatever you do, however, remember that *not* seasoning is not an option. While there may be people who need to restrict salt intake, restaurants that cook with little or no seasoning cannot turn out great cuisine. Much better to go light on the salt on request than to subject all your diners to the listless flavor of unseasoned food.

And now to that bête noire of the High Priests of Lightness: butter. This wonderful ingredient has gotten a bum rap in my opinion, largely because some French chefs of the mid-twentieth century would add butter and cream to everything—hoping to accomplish through richness what they may have lacked in ingredients, technique, or simply the time required for developing proper flavor. I have been gratified to note in recent years that scientists seem to have turned around on the questions of fat and butter. It seems that organically raised, grass-fed cows produce cream that is nutritious and not a recipe for a heart attack. The paradox for me, a French chef, is that the Italians use an enormous amount of butter, cream, and cheese in their pasta recipes and yet haven't been called out on the health hazards of those ingredients.

When a cook makes a simple piece of fish meunière, the heat of the lightly toasted butter spooned over the flesh gently warms the inside and imparts a light color to the outside. The result is a combination of the flavor punch that fat in the form of foamy browned butter, called *beurre noisette*, gives when properly used, a complex yet subtle transformation of the fish from a potentially bland filet to something spectacular and simple. By the way, have you ever had a lobster poached in butter by Thomas Keller at the French Laundry? It may not be on the menu anymore, but it is unforgettable. The lobster has a delicate, firm, and naturally sweet texture that is enhanced by poaching it in butter at a low temperature so the flavor is from-the-ocean fresh. The curve of heating is not aggressive; rather, it is gradual, primarily because butter is well suited to this method of cooking: firming the lobster yet maintaining moisture.

Do not be influenced by the faddish idea that butter does not belong in the kitchen. It's all about a very good quality butter used in moderation. Without it, you will never be able to cook many of the recipes in the *classique* repertoire. From simple croissants, pastry, and cookies to melted butter to *beurre blanc* to *beurre noisette* to *beurre noir*, there is a wide spectrum to this versatile and delicious ingredient. So, no, it is not something to resort to in order to add flavor when your culinary technique should have developed it in other ways, but yes, it is the pièce de résistance of so many recipes. Bear in mind that with popular modern techniques such as foaming (making a bubbly emulsion), butter does not have to equate with heaviness. It works on much the same principle that allows just a little bit of milk to produce a rich, frothy head on cappuccino, amplifying the coffee flavor. Often now in a restaurant you will find creative butters on the table with the bread—butters that incorporate smoked herbs, seaweed, citrus, and many more flavors.

Now to the spice rack and herb garden. These elements can be subtle or overpowering. Their character and strength vary with the ingredients they accompany. Slide a sprig of tarragon between the skin and breast meat of a chicken, and you will produce a slightly anise and minty bouquet that will dominate the more delicate flesh. In a béarnaise, however, pickled tarragon becomes an accent.

In my cooking—which, as I have said, is basically French— I tend to rely on the same dozen or so herbs. Each draws out the deeper layers of flavor in a dish, either by itself or in com- bination with others. Some, such as basil and tarragon, have a certain licorice quality that dramatizes a dish's sweetness. Somewhat different in effect, oregano, thyme, and sage help to frame and define more robust flavors. Take the example of a roast suckling pig. Its crisp, fatty skin and succulent meat create a chorus of aroma and flavor that will completely fill up every taste bud. To keep its flavor in proportion with others, adding oregano, thyme, and sage gives shape and definition and draws out the most savory aspects.

Parsley, and to an even greater degree watercress, have two separate but complementary aspects. One accents freshness, while the other—somewhere between bitterness and peppery sharpness—helps to contain a flavor and punctuate it (the way beer, for example, completely cleans off the palate and readies it for the next bite as if it were the first). In other words, rather than allowing flavor to accumulate and overwhelm, these herbs preserve the balance that otherwise could be tipped by a strong ingredient such as garlic. This is why in classical cooking parsley is often wedded to garlic.

When I first wrote these letters, the herbs mentioned above pretty much rounded out what was available in most restaurant kitchens, but the globalization that has occurred in recent years has not been confined to economics. Ingredients have been globalized as well: yuzu, cilantro, shiso, curry leaf, black garlic, and vadouvan reflect the contributions of other culinary cultures to the most basic European herbs available to contemporary chefs.

You must feel your way into these ingredients if you do not have a lifetime of tasting experience with them going all the way back to childhood. I think of the brilliant for-mer chef of Lespinasse, Gray Kunz, who dazzled New York diners all through the 1990s. Kunz grew up in Singapore, trained under Michelin-starred Frédy Girardet in Lausanne, then worked in Hong Kong for five years. Kunz had French technique and an intimate knowledge of the Eastern palate. His walleye pike with lavender-honey sauce and his rope mussels with lemongrass broth were examples of the finesse that comes from intimacy with ingredients, rather than the throw-it-all-in-the-pot-and-call-it-exotic approach of some chefs who like the idea of fusion cooking but have not rigorously studied it.

For myself, I like to imagine the flavor of a new ingredi-ent, then build from there. For example, I wanted to make a chilled velouté of oyster that would be creamy and briny, with subtle, unexpected, almost unidentifiable undertones. So I combined cream, oyster water, and heat to infuse the mixture with coriander seeds, lime peel, ginger, kaffir lime leaves, Thai basil, and lemongrass. Next, strain and chill. It's so floral and fragrant. Set an oyster afloat in it and you have an ensemble of the lightest, subtly complex flavors. I pick up the scent of the seacoast of Brittany alongside the mystery and sensuality of the Thai coast.

Aromatic spices such as cloves, cumin, anise, and curry (which is actually a mix of spices) also frame flavors beautifully as well as helping them punch through. Certain meats accept aromatics very well: pork, for example, and chicken (especially white meat). Aromatics give an instant identity to recipes, but as with everything, they should be used only in proportion. They can overwhelm with their strong perfume and slightly acrid flavor. The East and Middle East are justly famous for their aromatic spice mixes. They are as foundational to those cuisines as wine is to French, Spanish, or Italian gastronomy.

As I mentioned earlier, my global tour as a young chef pretty much began and ended in Denmark when Vergé sent me there to work at the Plaza Hotel in Copenhagen. Still, even this limited travel broadened me. I was captivated by Danish butter, bacon, and hams. Also aromatic cumin, caraway, rye seed, and dill seed. These are extremely good in marinades. What struck me while I was there was my love of cumin, an aromatic that really hits you with the first bite. But then its impact grows less noticeable until finally it recedes into the overall flavor of a recipe. In Mexico or Kerala I would also have come across cumin, but in those cornucopias of spices I might not have developed the more complete understanding of cumin that I got in Denmark.

Although it would be many years before the New Nordic movement would introduce the unique and enticing flavors of the fields, forests, and waters of Northern Europe to chefs all over the world, it is no doubt true that my background as a young chef in Denmark prepared me for the arrival of the subtleties of the Scandinavian palate in serious kitchens everywhere.

How you season—how you use butter or oil, herbs, and spices—is the signature of a chef, but it is of little use without the best ingredients. Finding the best and coaxing all the flavor out of them are subjects explored in my next letter.

SOURCES AND SEASONS

IN OUR GLOBALIZED world there are no more culinary back-waters, and any place you may find yourself working—from Manchuria to Madagascar—may one day contribute to the range of ingredients, tastes, and flavors at your command. Alex Atala, the Brazilian master, would go fly-fishing for golden dorado in the remote headwaters of the Bolivian Amazon because he liked to fish, but as a chef he could not help but be interested in the wild ingredients that the Tsimané Indians gathered in the rainforest. Those Amazonian ingredients have made him one of the most celebrated of modern chefs. Of course, he needed the foundation in technique that every chef must acquire through long years of study and practice, just as René Redzepi did before he stormed the world's Best Restaurant lists with the ingredients foraged in the Far North. But the success of these two contemporary masters has inspired a whole new generation to remain open to the boundless—and delicious—opportunities that lie in expanding one's knowledge of ingredients.

There can never be—has never been—a great restaurant with second-class ingredients. Whether it is as common as lettuce or as rarefied as white truffles or sushi-quality tuna, you must seek out the best. If you find yourself working for a chef who uses second-class ingredients, get out of there.

Of course, like everything else, pride in one's ingredients can be taken to extremes. In France, when I was young, there was a chef by the name of Thuilier. He was famous for his pride and for his volcanic temper. One day, the story goes, he was making the rounds in his dining room, and a patron complimented him on a wonderful dish but added, cluelessly, "It's too bad you couldn't find fresh green beans."

Incensed, Thuilier stormed into the kitchen, grabbed a crate of beautiful, fresh green beans, went back into the dining room, and emptied the entire contents on the table of the complaining diner. "Get out of my restaurant!" the chef ordered. "And do not ever come here again."

Thuilier was over the top, but his point is well taken. A great chef will not serve inferior ingredients. It follows, then, that a great chef will always seek out the best ingredients. Even if you have your own farm, a fishing boat, a platoon of hunters, and a personal forager, you won't be able to grow fruits in winter or find truffles in spring, catch shad in the summer or pick ramps in the fall. In other words, any chef is dependent on the seasons and his suppliers. A great supplier is as driven in his or her pursuit of the best as any great chef is. Purveyors, to use the term more common among chefs, are our connection to quality. Find these people and treat them like family. Feed them when they come to you. Send some cakes and cookies home for their kids. Spend time with them discussing their passion (that is, your ingredients).

A number of the top restaurants in New York get their poultry from a tiny dynamo of a woman named Sylvia Pryzant and her husband, Steve, a native of Manhattan's Yorkville. Though Sylvia's story is unusual, it is typical of many suppliers in that it is about arriving at a calling in life. She is a Tunisian Jew who was forced to leave her homeland in 1963. After passing her youth in Paris, she went to Israel, where she met her husband on a kibbutz. It proved difficult for her and Steve to get their own farm in Israel, so they came to the States and bought a farm in Pennsylvania, about three hours from Midtown Manhattan. They went into the business raising snow-white milk-fed veal. But they had absolutely no connections in the restaurant business.

That was no obstacle to Sylvia. She picked up the phone and called every top chef in town, until one of them (Tom Colicchio, who was the chef at Gramercy Tavern at the time) returned her call, tried her veal, and became a customer. With veal, Sylvia and Steve soon found that it is a long time between paychecks (it takes three months to raise a calf), so they decided to go into the milk-fed poultry business. There was only one problem. Nobody in America raised milk-fed poultry (which meant, in turn, that we chefs could never serve those wonderful *poulets de Bresse* that were available in France). But Sylvia was obsessed and would not stop until she learned the secret of the Bresse chicken, so she called Georges Blanc (my former mentor) in France and said, "Chef, what is the secret to raising these chickens?" Guess what? Blanc told her how to gradually change the chicken's diet from grain to milk pellets. Within a year, the top New York restaurants were serving milk-fed capon and their younger versions, the poularde and poussin.

Moral of the story: one Sylvia and one Steve Pryzant are worth two thousand everyday chicken farmers. So if you meet people who talk about the ingredients they offer with the same fond smile that others save for anecdotes about their children, get to know them. Try their product, and if it is good, treasure the people as you treasure the ingredients.

Another example is my friend Rod Mitchell. He comes from generations of Maine fishermen. His first career, though, was in the wine business, where he met Jean-Louis Palladin, the super-cool French chef who brought me to America. It was Jean-Louis who convinced Rod that there was a market for hand-harvested diver scallops. Rod was the first person I heard of to offer these succulent, super-fresh, and sweet morsels. On a visit to Maine, Jean-Louis, acting on a hunch, took a net down to the river and hauled in some small eels (*piballes*), one of the favorite fish ingredients of the southwest of France. With no bones to speak of, they are an unforgettable delicacy when served with nothing more than Espelette peppers, olive oil, and garlic. Jean-Louis urged Rod to begin supplying French restaurants with these baby American eels, and Rod took up the challenge. As a result, we have access to an ingredient we might never have had were it not for a friendship between chef and supplier.

Of course, Rod's seafood sometimes costs more than regular fish from a local market. But it is not surprising. He gets me wild Copper River salmon in the summer, as deeply pink as lobster coral. Closer to home he finds fresh cod, halibut, skate . . . the best of the ocean. These things cost more, which brings me to another important point: buy the best ingredients you can afford.

Basically, there have been two cuisines for which the price of ingredients has not been a controlling factor: French and Japanese. In Paris you can charge $450 for dinner and, if you are Alain Passard, you may have a full house every night. In Japan, Sukiyabashi Jiro has a tiny little sushi house at the entry to a subway station, and people wait months to snag a reservation for a $300 omakase (chef-selected) meal featuring the best toro, prized mackerel known as aji, and plump live shrimp.

With those cuisines, as with yours, clientele and imagination determine what ingredients you should buy and can afford to buy. It does not all have to be truffles, foie gras, and caviar. It can be blood-red heirloom tomatoes, hand-foraged field greens, crisp October apples. Still, to develop a great restaurant you will occasionally have to shell out for the expensive stuff. Just find a way to be sure you can sell it and that you use every shaving of truffle, every last caviar egg, every slice of foie gras. Waste is always the restaurateur's enemy, doubly so when the ingredients are as expensive as gold. As a growing movement among chefs has shown, often the stuff that we think of as waste can be the basis of nutritious meals. If you don't want it for your restaurant, there are food kitchens that will be happy to convert your cast-offs into meals that sustain hungry people who don't have the resources of your clientele.

I grew up on a farm where we ate what we grew. It could not have been more seasonal, and ever since, I have carried with me that affection for seasonality as part of my culinary DNA. It is my ruling passion. For nine months of the year we never ate a zucchini, but when they were in season, we made something with them almost every day. In fall, we had crisp, tart apples and sweet, musky pears that we stored under the top couple of inches of barley in our silo. The fruits would slowly ripen and keep for three months, well into winter. So yes, we did eat them "out of season," I suppose, but we preserved them at their peak of flavor.

It is flavor peakness that makes seasonality so important to ingredients. Spring is the wakening earth, summer its sweet season, fall a time of ripeness. All of us, not just chefs, can't help but think this way. Seen in this light, ingredients connect us in the most basic way to the rhythm of the planet.

When a new season comes, I return to my favorite dishes for that time of year, but I find it is also a time to challenge oneself to create new dishes. That is one of the lovely mysteries of cuisine, how seeing an ingredient for the first time each year somehow spurs one to create. Listen to your inner chef; it will tell you that the fava beans before you need a baby-carrot coulis alongside some poached crayfish. Or it will tell you that a gnarly Hubbard squash you've found in the market is incomplete until filled with black walnuts, fennel sausage, Macoun apples, and a lacing of Calvados.

There was a time when I believed that the best ingredients (and therefore the only ones worth using) were those that could be trucked in. In Lyon, in my boyhood, this was certainly true. Within driving distance, the fruit and vegetables would ripen in the fields and orchards and be at their absolute peak. The fish would be a few hours from the sea, the cheeses just a day's drive from the aging caves in the mountains.

For the most part, I still like to cook that way. To be sure, I can get amazing cherries from Chile in December. By the same token, I can also go swimming in a heated pool in New York in December—but somehow neither the swimming nor the cherries seem connected with the season, and for that reason I find them out of place.

As the child of a farm I know very well that there are times when there aren't many fresh fruits and vegetables on the farm to bring to the table. In February, I'd have trouble making an interesting restaurant meal that clients would pay for with fresh, local products from our farm in St. Pierre! That's a tall order. So while farm-to-table is often the mantra of modern food activists, and we chefs want to come down on the right side of environmental and food issues, it also bears reminding ourselves that wholesome, nutritious, and delicious fruits and vegetables *always* come from a farm somewhere in the world. Sometimes as important as the miles something travels are the answers to the questions "Is the farmer environmentally responsible, and is the food harvested or slaughtered in a responsible/humane way?" If the answers are yes, I don't have a problem resorting to more remote suppliers when there is nothing local to be had. In other words, I am not above "pushing" the seasons: getting peaches from the Carolinas in June or sweet corn from Florida. The suppliers load them on an eighteen-wheeler—hot from the orchard or field—and we have them three days later, beautifully ripe. Or I can call my mushroom supplier from Oregon and have chanterelles picked one day and in my prep kitchen the next. Because of modern transportation, these foods are still seasonal—at their peak—and still have a relation to the season in New York.

In the modern larder not everything is local in any season, so I do not need to feel a seasonal connection to cook with certain ingredients. Passion fruits are completely exotic to me, so I can cook with them any time of the year without feeling that I am breaking my connection to the season. I used to feel this way about pineapples, but in recent years we have begun to see golden Hawaiian pineapples that are tender and fairly bursting with juice. Now I tend to wait to cook with pineapples until I see the golden ones in the market.

In addition to fruits and vegetables, fish, fowl, and meat have seasons as well. Again, I try to stay in tune with my local season or at least the spirit of the season. Spring lamb from the hills of eastern Pennsylvania, Gardiners Bay scallops in October, shad from the Delaware in May, Scottish grouse in August, Delaware duck and goose in the fall, upstate New York venison in early winter.

If you are in tune with the seasons, you will dream about cooking with a particular ingredient when you can find it readily in the market. Stay with the seasons and you cannot go wrong. You will be, as the saying goes, "happy as God in France." And if you have ever been in a French market full of the choice offerings of the season—bounteous, exploding with flavor, a palette of deep colors to inspire an artist—you will understand why God is so happy. P.S. These days, when I consider ingredients, I think God could be pretty happy in Barcelona, Tuscany, and upstate New York, too.

This could be a good arena in which to become a bit more activist or political, à la Alice Waters or David Chang. Why should a young chef care? Because as a head chef or owner of a restaurant, you are part of a community. Many communities today lack good access to fresh, unprocessed, healthful ingredients, and chefs have a certain expertise in this realm. Giving back to your community will drive the community back to you.

WINE AND PASTRY

LET'S CONSIDER ECONOMICS. When you have your own restaurant and start to review your accounting, you will see that savory foods—the items that come from the garde-manger to the hot lines—account for a little bit more than half the average check. About 10 to 15 percent of that check is generated by the pastry department, and approximately a third goes to the wine cellar. So it is absolutely critical that the complete chef be very conversant with wine and pastry.

Let's take those economics a bit further. Although wine is just 30 to 40 percent of the business's overall sales, the profit margin on it is often much higher. Sometimes with liquor it's double the profit of the food. This is not, as many people think, because we mark up the bottles 200 or 300 percent. The important thing is to invest in wines that are relatively inexpensive when they are released but that will become more and more valuable as the years go by.

Today, we have to be especially creative with our wine program. Prices for fine wine have escalated to a point where the consumer is both very cautious and very knowledgeable. We try to buy in quantities that will allow us to sometimes negotiate a better deal and keep the wines at reasonable prices on our lists. We are always very attentive to auctions where, occasionally, we can "steal" a wine by acting very quickly and aggressively. We also have developed relationships with private collectors who occasionally "thin out" their cellars and come to us first. Good relationships and fast payments help!

Sometimes the profit margin on wine is reduced, because there is no guarantee that a bottle will not be corked. You must also figure in capital costs, the price of storage, interest foregone had you left the money in the bank—and God forbid a bottle be knocked off the shelf as a frantic waiter hurries to satisfy a demanding customer. And, finally, there is always the risk of what happens should the economy tank.

A great wine list will attract a great clientele, one that knows the value of wine and is willing to indulge. The quality of your wine list will bear a direct and significant impact on your average check in two ways. The wine itself contributes directly to the check. Moreover, the diner who will pay gladly for an Haut-Brion or a Chateau Montelena will expect only the finest food ingredients—the truffles, the grouse, the wild salmon, the porcini. The decision to buy these ingredients in affordable quantities means you will have enough so that you can also offer them to the folks who are buying the less costly bottle of wine. The same relationship holds true in gastropubs or casual places that are chef- or sommelier-driven. There are always some customers who will order the more expensive bottles of wine. When they do it helps you to rebuild your stock faster.

Vintage Bordeaux represents the big time in collectibles and investment. Then there is Burgundy, the premium Italians, the California cult wines, the prime picks from Mendoza or Australia—you must have a list that represents these categories. Burgundy produces so little wine compared to the demand for it that the prices are driven up. Although it is important for a gastronomic restaurant to have that Latour '61 or '70 for the customer who wants the best and does not care about price, it is just as important for your reputation to offer newer, lesser-known winemakers and less costly bottles. For example, I take greater pride in finding some of Jim Clendenen's Sanford and Benedict pinot noir than in buying a '78 Corton, which is already well known to every oenophile. Someday the young producers are going to become the old masters, and, of equal importance, you will have diners who want good wine but do not have the pocketbook for the pricey stuff. Those customers are your future, and you cannot afford to drive them away with the sticker shock of a Greatest Hits wine list.

As a young chef you will have many opportunities to broaden your knowledge of wine. These days, there are tastings all around town (not only in New York, but in any serious restaurant town). There also is a tremendous depth of information contained in books, newspapers, magazines, and food and wine festivals. Still, there is no substitute for tasting. Just watch how much you taste. I remember at one of my early jobs, we had one old chef—a good chef at that—who was pretty lit five days out of six. That will not fly anymore.

You have advantages that I didn't when I started. Being French, we accepted wine as part of life, but if we had to drive somewhere to get it, my dad's philosophy was, Why bother? He was a man of very local mentality. Like most Frenchmen, we drank the wine of our region, northern Rhônes and southern Burgundies: thick, sun-rich syrah; crisp, delicate yet powerful pinot noir. It wasn't until I worked in a fancy restaurant in Lyon that I began to learn about Bordeaux. Whereas the Burgundies and Rhônes of my youth were a pure expression of *terroir* (the land, the climate, and the *je ne sais quois* that define a wine region), Bordeaux often has more elegance and powerful lightness.

At my next job, at Georges Blanc, on our days off we would try the wines of Mâconnais and Beaujolais, and regional wines such as those of Provence and the Loire—wines that are good for everyday consumption, are affordable, and are very representative of the wide range of wines in the French bistro tradition. We would visit winemakers, driving all day from village to village, and to tell the truth, by five in the afternoon we were feeling toasty. But we were young, and that is the way young chefs were (and still are). Nowadays many chefs travel with their sommeliers to the wine country.

At my restaurants, we encourage kitchen staff to learn about wine and to attend classes on wine, or to come to tastings directed by the sommeliers. I will see those same faces at wine tastings that I see bent over their notebooks jotting down recipes in the kitchen, or spending their down time asking other cooks about ingredients, techniques, and so on. It boils down to this: the young chef who has ambitions to be a great chef is interested in every aspect of the business, and wine is a very big aspect.

Apart from being a companion to food, wine is a primary ingredient in French cuisine. It is fundamental to Italian, German, Spanish, and modern American cooking too. Wine helps to balance acidity and concentrate and enrich flavor in a way that vinegar or lemon juice or beer cannot. Only wine has the complexity to bring out the length of flavor in a sauce bordelaise for a ribeye steak, or in a *civet de lapin,* or in a poularde in a creamy Riesling sauce.

Asian, Middle Eastern, and Latin American cuisines did not evolve around wine the way European cuisine has. Spices, herbs, chilies, and fermented ingredients other than wine were the traditional backbones of these rich traditions.

As these cuisines have made their way into the mainstream of first-class modern restaurants, chefs are inventing beverage pairings that are outside the European canon but exciting in their own way for the new possibilities they open up. They will pair foods with cocktails, beer, sake, or booze—no longer just wine.

Whatever beverage you are pairing with your food, there is something magical about wine that I cannot put into words. Perhaps wine is sacramental because it is touched with an aura of the mystical and sacred. Certainly the French treat it that way. I remember my parents telling me stories of the war, when every family hid their wine from the enemy. The invaders could take other things, but *never* would they take our wine! From the great châteaux of Bordeaux to the hills of Côte-Rôtie and even in my own home, wine was hidden like the family jewels. My grandfather Joseph Boulud dug a secret underground bunker in which to hide our wine. In our case, it was not about the value of the wine as something collectible but rather the value of the wine as something the family held and loved to share. Wine was part of our patrimony.

Wine, then, is the essence of the French dining experience. So are the wonderful sugary caprices that pour out of the pastry kitchen, although there are no stories of families hiding treasure troves of pastry in their cellars. Everybody loves pastry, and even the most health-conscious diners usually indulge in something rich and sweet for dessert when they go out for a special occasion. They do not do this every night at home, but when they come to a fine restaurant they usually think, "Why not? One pear clafoutis won't push me up three belt notches."

Gastronomically, dessert is important. The palate craves sweetness at the end of a meal. There is something warm and cozy about dessert, like a goodnight kiss from Mom before she would tuck you in at night. As mentioned above, this childhood craving that stays with grownup diners will account for 10 to 15 percent of the check. Although food costs for desserts are relatively low, labor costs can run high—especially if you have an especially experienced or artistic pastry chef. Still, I believe it is worthwhile to have a well-paid pastry chef because well-conceived, well-executed, and well-marketed desserts can be twice as profitable as your main courses and appetizer. That is a huge hunk of business, one that you cannot afford to leave to the printed menu and hope that the customer takes the hint. These days, when everyone is counting calories and many share desserts, you need to reawaken people's appetites with a special dessert menu while making sure that your waitstaff is trained in describing the sweets in the most tantalizing manner.

For your own foundation as a chef, you must acquire an understanding of baking (both bread and pastry). It is much easier to do this when you are younger rather than waiting until the responsibilities of the kitchen pile up on you. Just like the eager-to-learn chef who comes to our wine tastings, the young chef who spends an afternoon every now and then with the pastry chef or bread baker is the person I recognize as having the drive and ambition to advance in this business.

Although pastry and the rest of the menu both come out of the kitchen, and all are made by a brigade wearing checked pants and white coats, they are two very different disciplines. Cooking is often about speed and creativity in technique. It is also about the ability to improvise—to accommodate variations in ingredients—while maintaining consistency in the finished product. Pastry is the opposite. It is less about spontaneous creativity and more about precision and measuring. Instead of speed, it is about waiting. Pastry ingredients—flour, sugar, butter, sometimes chocolate—are much more uniform than the basic ingredients in appetizers and main courses. In a way, pastry is more like chemistry, whereas the rest of cooking is rather like music. Both have a written-out plan, but in baking you rarely deviate, and in cooking you often must change and adapt.

The creativity of the pastry chef often expresses itself in elaborate presentation and delicious combinations. If, as they say, first impressions are important, last impressions are equally so in a restaurant. It is hard for the customer to forget a mille-feuille (literally translated as a thousand sheets) of parchment-thin layers of extra-bitter Venezuelan chocolate separating wafers of toasted hazelnut praline, held together by multilevels of pillowy-soft arabica coffee mousse and crowned with a zabaglione of smoky Kentucky bourbon. Crunchy, toasty, bitter, sweet, mildly intoxicating, and thoroughly seductive.

You may never be a pastry chef, but you cannot call yourself a chef at all if you have not mastered the art of making dough. It is basic to desserts, but also to many of the things we do with hot and cold savory appetizers as well as with main courses. For example, *brioche, pâte sablée,* and puff pastry are used as much in savory items as in sweet. A combination of crayfish, morels, sweetbreads, and asparagus in a foamy chervil sauce on a flaky, golden pastry crust is a far cry from a tart of crushed fresh figs tossed with cinnamon and brown sugar and baked over a butter-rich crust. Still, they both depend on mastering the delicate and demanding art of puff pastry. So even though you may have little interest in becoming a pastry chef because you have your sights set on the line, spending some time on the dough station will serve you well.

Did you ever watch a pastry chef draw a picture of a dessert? It is almost like watching an architect. You are struck with the physical design, how flavor is located in different layers, the way texture enters into the equation. Whereas a line cook might rely more on gut and inspiration, the pastry chef always plans it out. Many line cooks I have known would have benefited from this kind of planning. No doubt I have such respect for the pastry chef because Michel Guérard, my mentor, and Alex Stupak, of Alinea and WD-50, were pastry chefs before they decided to become chefs. Their visual artistry and creativity, by virtue of their pastry background, are beyond the capability of most traditional chefs.

Although I can think of nothing more perfect than a classic chocolaty and creamy éclair washed down with a cup of espresso, at the same time, I will never say no to some just-invented passion-fruit extravaganza topped with a scoop of saffron gelato. One is not better than the other, and whether you want to create traditional or original desserts you must understand the basic principles of pastry and desserts as they are practiced by pastry chefs. Then you must learn to let your imagination go. As I write this I cannot help but think of one of my former pastry chefs, Dominique Ansel. Where did he get the insane idea of marrying a donut and a croissant? Certainly not from the traditions of classic pastry. Instead it was a bolt of playful inspiration from his genius that led him to pair two iconic pastries, French and American, into one that produced lines of hundreds of people waiting outside his Manhattan, London, Tokyo, and LA shops.

I mentioned earlier how I am interested in exploring all the facets of the flavor profile of an ingredient. Right now at Bar Boulud we are making a strawberry, lime, and rhubarb dessert. In a glass, layer a light lime gelée, a mix of fresh and stewed strawberries, a tart lime whipped cream, strawberry granita, and rhubarb ice cream. Alongside we serve a warm rhubarb turnover. Three basic ingredients (rhubarb, lime, and strawberry) presented in a multitude of texture and taste.

Without the knowledge of how to use sugar precisely, how to create sweetened creams, and how to layer elements, this would be a so-so dessert, the kind that kids make when they dump every sweet thing in the refrigerator into a mixing bowl. Only by virtue of the fact that we have studied the science of sweetness and tartness in pastry as well as in basic cuisine can we get to an interesting and novel "chef's dessert." And if there is ever a place where pure whimsy and caprice rule on the menu, it is in the desserts.

THE WHOLE WIDE WORLD

EXPERIENCING OTHER CUISINES in their home territory is more important for a chef today than it ever was. It will be even more so in the future, because many chefs have learned across the globe and then gone back to their homeland to create a new cuisine with their indigenous ingredients. But before you buy your tickets and take off for Lima or Sri Lanka, there are some things you need to ask yourself.

First, what kind of food interests you? Italian, French, Peruvian, Chinese, Mexican, Indian, Thai, Japanese? If you have an idea of what you particularly like, it can be an indication of what cuisines you ought to see and try. You do not always have to travel the world, by the way. In New York City, you could sample at least thirty different cuisines—in true ethnic communities—if you hopped on the number 7 train at Grand Central and got off at every stop in Queens.

You will find restaurants, groceries, butchers, bakers, fish stores—all specializing in ethnic ingredients.

New York is not America's only melting pot. San Francisco, New Orleans, Los Angeles, and Chicago all have ethnic communities: Vietnamese, Italian, Mexican, Japanese, Eastern European, Portuguese, and others. So you can do a lot of your culinary world traveling close to home. The important thing is that you try the real thing—true cuisines—wherever you can find them.

Even for the explorer who does not have access to the real thing, we are all floating on a sea of cookbooks, magazines, documentaries, YouTube videos, and Instagram posts crammed with recipes and mouth-watering pictures of different world cuisines. Any food magazine or even the food section of any international paper will pretty much take you around the world if you read it for a year.

We did not have such a wide exposure to global cuisine when I was a young chef. Honestly, we didn't think we needed it. I understand why we thought that way. We were French, and the French all think that serious cuisine is French cuisine. French is the language of cuisine the way English is the language of air traffic control. I say that because in France, even in small, remote villages, you can find a great chef who is cooking local cuisine or who has a world reputation. Clearly, today any country can claim world-class talent, but maybe not yet all over the country, the way France can.

I have since come to learn that things are not so simple. At the same time, it is indisputable that the modern restaurant is a French invention; the "software"—that is, the way a restaurant is organized—is likewise French. And nowhere else have chefs taken a national cuisine and refined it so much and as variedly as have the French. As I mentioned earlier, part of the explanation is that France in the latter part of the eighteenth century was the first country to develop true restaurants: establishments that offered a varied bill of fare, set prices, and the ability to order à la carte. As restaurants advanced, a culture evolved with them. Cuisine held a rank alongside theater and the other arts. The result was a public that would pay the price for the best food and challenge their chefs to new heights of creativity.

The French took dining, a part of daily life, raised it to an art, embedded it in high culture, and thereby attracted the economic resources necessary to develop a more refined and expert interpretation of food than anywhere else in the world. In much the same way, French haute couture took another part of daily life and developed it. A dress embroidered with pearls and trimmed with fur is, in some sense, not unlike a saddle of veal studded with truffles, stuffed with porcini and chestnuts, and glazed with ruby port. It is expensive. It is refined. But it would never happen were it not for a public that appreciated and would pay for it. Cultures make choices for their definitive statements. The Italians lavished everything on developing their opera and the Russians their ballet. The French chose haute cuisine and haute couture. Today these two *hautes* have gone global yet have kept their French sensibility.

Even in France, however, chefs have learned to include North African and Indochinese culinary traditions (maybe the only good result of colonialism). When Alain Senderens made his reputation in the 1970s as one of the most innovative chefs in the nouvelle cuisine movement, he had a young Cambodian in the kitchen, Sottha Khun (my good friend and former executive chef at Le Cirque), who could tell him if the new Asian flavors he was trying rang true. I do not know where Senderens got his inspiration for combining lobster and vanilla bean, but it certainly came from outside the canon of Parisian cuisine. It was one of the defining recipes of nouvelle cuisine, and I suspect it emerged from the fact that with all the international influences included in his food, he was open to the strangest yet most delicate combinations.

When I started out, the Lyonnais regarded themselves as residents of the self-titled world's food capital. Even if you didn't agree with them, you could see why they thought so. If you drew a ring around Lyon a hundred miles from the center, Place Bellecour, you would probably have encircled more Michelin stars than anywhere else in the world, including Paris. So the grand tour of the world's cuisines was not such a big thing with us.

Still, after a short while in the business, I yearned to see something new, anything. When I was sixteen, I told Nandron that I wanted to take a summer vacation. Like a true French chef, he replied, "You do not need a vacation, for God's sake; you are sixteen years old! I'll get you a job at my friend's auberge in the Pays Basque."

So I left my home region for the first time and worked for three months at a restaurant in the most remote corner of southwestern France (in the Hotel Etchola in the little village of Ascain). Same country, but what a revelation! The trout just about jumped into your bucket from the mountain streams of the Pyrénées. There were the heavenly Ossau Iraty cheeses made from sheep's milk that grazed on sweet mountain grasses! And the Jambon de Bayonne, wild mushrooms, and invigorating Espelette peppers were all new and exciting to me. I immediately learned the importance to a young chef of being open to other cuisines. *Hybrid vigor* is the term used in agriculture to describe how the offspring of two genetic strains is often more robust than either parent; the same is true in cooking.

If I were your age, I would think about a trip to France, Spain, Italy, or Scandinavia—those countries offer the richest and most innovative European cuisines, in my opinion. Eat everywhere you can. Go to the markets, the wineries, the food shops. If you can find a position, then by all means get a *stage* (internship) or cook's job for six months.

Pay attention to your family's traditions as well. My real point is that coming at things through the focus of culinary tradition allows you to create with confidence.

Apart from Europe and its culinary offspring in the States, India and Mexico both offer varied regional cuisines, tremendous refinement, and novel (to a European palate) ways of combining flavors and textures. China, too, has a rich culinary tradition, and even though it would be hard to claim that I think of myself as a young chef at this point, I learned from opening and operating restaurants there. Its imperial cuisine did for the indigenous cuisine what French gastronomy did for our home cuisines. In contrast, Singapore, although a young city, offers an Asian food culture ranging from the street to the refined table.

Peru has wonderful cuisine. I love its ceviches, and with the large influence of Japanese culture, it has wonderful sushi as well. You could not think of a better place to learn about raw fish and marinades than Peru, or to draw on Incan influences and the ingredients of the Andes the way Virgilio Martínez and Gastón Acurio have. Argentina has a reputation for the best meat in the world, and in our Netflix *Chef's Table* era there are would-be Francis Mallmanns cooking with wood fires all around the globe.

The cuisines of the Middle East are as rich as any, with a sophisticated use of aromatic spices. Chefs such as Yotam

Ottolenghi and Michael Solomonov have done much to bring this influence into modern restaurant kitchens. A trip to Israel will take you to an exciting scene of culinary innovation. Then, of course, there is Vietnamese food, for which we French chefs have a special fondness. Before the word *fusion* had anything to do with food, French chefs were marrying their techniques with the ingredients and recipes of this ancient and elegant cuisine. The result was multicultural and refined.

Any place in Indochina—Thailand, Laos, Burma—will offer you a great cooking tradition with more exotic-looking fruits and vegetables and more varied seafood than you would have thought possible. And the region is so sensual, with its spices, flowers, temples, and tropical air.

Take six months to two years. Travel the world, work with chefs everywhere you can, eat every kind of food. And then get ready for the rude awakening when you return home and begin a job at a top restaurant. It could be with Michael Anthony's Gramercy Tavern, Barbara Lynch's Menton, or Paul Kahan's Blackbird. Nobody is going to care all that much that you have been to Italy or Singapore or Shanghai because their main concern is only how well you can cook their food. They'll look at your résumé, check your references, and look you in the eye, and if you are lucky they will hire you. When that happens, your immediate task in life is no longer to dream about foreign cuisines and faraway temples. What matters now is the clatter and heat of a real kitchen and a chef who wants it his or her way.

So nourish your culinary soul with a world tour when you have the chance, and continue to nourish it with Sunday trips to restaurants or trying out new cookbooks. Frankly, you may not have the time or pocketbook to travel and take jobs here and there, but you can still let your imagination roam. This will give you greater perspective as a chef and will somehow seep into your ideas and techniques.

Fantasy world versus real world: this is the dichotomy customers make when they choose your restaurant for a night. And it is what keeps us all going in the kitchen when the orders back up, tempers flare, waiters mix up their tables, soufflés fall . . . you name it.

Soak up all you can now; then it is time to start building your career.

DESIRE, DRIVE, AND FOCUS

I HAD A young chef come to me one day who had been doing a great job at garde manger. He wanted to move onto the line as a cook, which is pretty true to form for any aspiring chef. So we moved him to poissonier (the fish station), and right away you could see his lack of experience, speed, and productivity. We had to watch over him, to use the French phrase, *comme le lait sur le feu* (like milk on the fire). In other words, we would have to watch him very carefully to make sure he did not suddenly upset the entire service by over-cooking, oversalting, charring, forgetting an ingredient, lack of coordination, or making other errors that can ruin a recipe so quickly.

Don't be in a hurry to move up the restaurant ladder. There is a lot to absorb at every station. Moving you before you are ready does no favor to you or the rest of the kitchen brigade. You will always be playing catch-up, and they will always be waiting on you. It's really much better for everyone, yourself included, to become as expert as you can at every step of the way. It takes time, but once you move up, unless you really screw up, you are not going to have the opportunity to go back and fill in the gaps in your skills.

Although something may look easy, often the subtleties of everything you do in the kitchen require long practice and careful observation. Mastering the simple technique of controlling heat on the stovetop will take time. As many restaurants do, we have a series of metal rings that cover each burner: by moving the pot closer to or further from that heat epicenter, you can get temperatures over 800°F or as low as a lazy simmer. Young cooks will get the hang of it, but they have to observe everything by watching their chefs. If they have the talent and are driven, the day will come in the not too distant future when they can master the heat.

Just be prepared for the chef to throw you a curve. They all do. When I had maybe a year under my belt at my first job, my boss, after a week of hunting in Alsace, arrived in his Citroën DS 21 (the French Cadillac) and opened the trunk, which was full of game: pheasants, hares, partridges, woodcocks. All were going on the menu for that night, and I had to get them ready for service. Two other guys and I spent the whole afternoon plucking birds, dressing them, and learning six new recipes to create a wild-game feast. I had cooked game that my family and I had shot, but now, in a serious restaurant, new combinations of ingredients were coming at me from every direction. We had pheasant terrine, partridge chartreuse, woodcock *flambé à l'Armagnac* with croutons spread with crushed woodcock giblets and butter. And *lièvre à la royale*—boneless wild hare stuffed with foie gras truffles and ground pork, braised till spoon tender in a concentrated red wine, blood, and hare stock. So much to learn and do so fast. I had to run like crazy to stay up with the service and not make any mistakes.

Of course, these kinds of surprises are not the rule. Most restaurant work is endless repetition of simple techniques. Let me give you an idea of the day you can look forward to at one of my restaurants or David Chang's or Marcus Samuelsson's—it doesn't matter whose, because the work is the same. Let's say you are at my restaurant, DANIEL. We are not open for lunch there, so if you are a cook, you will come at noon and may stay until late at night.

Sometime in the next ten hours, you can count on me or the sous chef or whoever is above you to get on your case pretty hard. Get used to it. You have to worry when your chef is *not* constantly on your case. No one would waste their time if they didn't think you had something going for you. That's probably small consolation when you're getting chewed out for overcooking a halibut, but in all honesty that's about as close as you'll ever get to winning a medal in many kitchens. In a kitchen, praise is the absence of criticism.

Through the course of the day you'll have a couple of breaks and a meal or two, but between one o'clock and five thirty you are getting prepared, doing your *mise en place*. If you have talent, discipline, speed, and focus, you will get through this quickly. If you are new on the station, you may have good habits and focus, but there is no way that you can work at the same pace as an experienced chef. In that event, you will need to improve fast with a smart game plan because it will take time to get up to speed. We will give you the drill of what you have to do and how you should do it—how to shell a pea very quickly, how to debone a squab rapidly, how to mince shallots into microdice—but then your level of skill and your preplanning take over.

I had one prep cook, Chepe, who could go through three cases of peas by the time a young cook had done a few pounds. I do not expect the young cook to be as quick as Chepe. I cannot even describe how he did it. It is one of those things experts do in a blur of hands and a pile of pods. But a smart young cook, when given the job, would watch Chepe for a while, then put his or her observations to work.

Skill and planning ahead take practice. Every skill takes practice, including the skill of knowing how much you have to do. Though you may have the technical aspects of *mise en place* down, if you have not figured out how much is required, you will either waste time or mess up the smooth flow of service by doing too much or too little prep. Wasted motion in the kitchen has a time cost, often as disruptive as insufficient preparation. By looking at the reservations, the number of portions available, the semipredictable habits of the clientele, you should know exactly what you need to do to be ready.

Doing all these things correctly in the midst of the many demands of a first-rate kitchen requires aggressiveness, concentration, and, most of all, stamina. Your job is to work rapidly with precision and consistency.

In prep or service we do not have time to slow down, so the only way to get up to speed is to invest your free time in honing your skill, spending time with the men and women who are the best at each particular task. Then, as you concentrate and practice, it gets easier and you can relax. This is not to say that the work gets easier, but the pressure lifts as you become more accomplished and organized, planning your day according to what you need to get done and the level of your ability—always remembering that in addition to the one task you are trying to master, there are five or six others that you will be called upon to finish at the same time!

I remember in Vergé's kitchen having to prep *mousseron* mushrooms and baby artichokes on the same morning. Both were included in popular items on the menu, so there were mountains of them. The baby artichokes required force, speed, and an adept knife hand to peel away the tough outer layers. It was a mean job. The tiny cap mushrooms, though, required more delicacy and a lighter touch to trim the stem. Two different skills, neither of them ones you naturally possess just by picking up a knife. I can still hear Vergé's direction to his troops, which comprised his entire employee-motivation scheme: *Plus vite, encore plus vite.* Faster, and then even faster. But I was doing it as fast as I could.

The bottom line is the only way you will advance in this profession is if you invest your own time over and above your time on the clock. If you are driven to be a chef, this will not be an issue. I suppose the same is true for orchestra conductors, race car drivers, surgeons, and ballerinas. Every profession that draws ambitious dreamers demands time. It will come naturally to you because your interest and your desire will constantly propel you to the kitchen. And when you are done with your current task, you will be peppering the sous chef on the next station with questions. You can't help it. It is in your blood. It does not make the time commitment easier or leave you any less tired at the end of the day, but people who are driven by something—or better yet, drawn irresistibly to a goal—do not count being tired as a bad thing.

When the day comes that you have mastered one station, your chef will move you to another. Hopefully, it will not come as a complete novelty, because you have been interested in and observant of the rest of the kitchen. Still, when you have to take on the next job, you will start all over again, knowing next to nothing and not even doing that particularly well. But if you put in the time and have the desire, you will learn and we will teach you.

You must look inside yourself and find desire, because if you have it then you will make the time sacrifices and endure the criticism. Although I will never deny that it is hard work to become a chef, the clatter of the kitchen, the intense aromas, the mix of languages, the precision teamwork of the kitchen brigade when the service is really rocking . . . all these things make me feel alive and charged in a way that nothing else can. So yes, you work until you are bone tired, but there is nothing else you would rather do. Is that any different from a tennis player who wants to make it to Wimbledon or a guitarist whose ambition is to play Madison Square Garden?

One more requirement—you need youth. Notice these are letters to a *young* chef, not a *new* chef. In other words, if you were forty years old I would not be writing this to you, because the demands of the job and the competition in the restaurant world require stamina and energy—two qualities that you have when you are younger but that lessen as you grow older. This is as true of chefs as it is of basketball players or Olympic swimmers. Youth is one of your few advantages; put it to good use. It is best to start young in this career, though as I write this advice, I remember that Chef Thuilier in Provence, whose famous volcanic temper I described earlier, was a successful insurance broker in Paris until, at age fifty, he moved down south and opened Les Baux de Provence. But he is the exception. Since he lived into his late eighties, he had as long a run as a top chef (Michelin three-star) as anyone in the business.

But back to you, my young friend. Every newcomer I have ever known who went on to become an accomplished chef kept a diary of techniques and recipes and a small collection of "holy books." I still have my tattered copy of Gringoire and Saulnier's *Le répertoire de la cuisine,* which was my version of CliffsNotes for cooks, full of the basics of recipes and definitions of terms. If the chef asked me to cut something *paysanne* style, instead of scratching my head and wondering how on earth a peasant would cut things, I looked it up in *Le répertoire* and found that it means large, rustic pieces.

Going back to your original sources and inspirations is something you will do throughout your career. You'd be surprised how much "old stuff" remains true. As a chef you join countless generations of chefs—both at home and in the restaurant kitchen. You are the transmitter of millennia of food culture, and people come to you with an emotional expectation as well as a culinary one. Your customers trust you to make their celebration as special as the feelings that go with it. That trust makes you realize fully that being a chef is indeed a high calling.

ATTITUDE AND TEAMWORK

NOT EVERYTHING IN the career of a chef fits into tidy pigeon-holes. In this letter I would like to offer you a grab bag of qualities, essential but disparate, that I have observed in young cooks who went on to become top-flight chefs in their own right. It all starts with self-management and good attitude.

Some cooks are meticulous in classifying recipes, keeping track of all the details in the kitchen that contribute to a dish. I have found that such cooks can often be successful and manage well. I remember from my early days that the chefs who did this were the ones who went on to bigger things. We would get together after work or on days off to compare notes from our diaries and exchange recipes. Remember, back then, well before the digital age of online recipes and cooking shows, our mentors (Vergé, Chapel, Haeberlin, and so on) did not have their own cookbooks. Often during our afternoon breaks we would trade recipes the way kids trade baseball cards: "Hey, I'll give you three Bocuses for two Vergé and a Girardet." You would never get this exchange at the top level—one great chef to another—so this is how valuable "chef DNA" would get mixed, and the result would be ideas for new dishes that were in a sense the offsprings of the top chefs of the day.

If you have a deep interest in recipes, it often follows that you understand how to begin to organize the details of a recipe. These are tremendously revealing qualities, because only through understanding the details and organization of a recipe can you achieve consistency, the hallmark of a good kitchen. If I do a terrine of foie gras and there are fifteen cooks and assistants in the kitchen, I look for the person who asks me detailed and insightful questions about the recipe. He or she really wants to understand. The others? They do their jobs. They may do them well, maybe better than the one who asked the question, but still I think the inquiring chef is the one who, once he or she understands a recipe, will be *consistent*. Remember that word, underline it, put it on your mirror to look at every day.

People may visit your restaurant once because it sounds interesting. They may visit it a second time because they had a very good meal the first time, but they will only keep coming back if the food and service are consistent. The goal of the chef, whatever the level of cuisine, is consistency. Consistency in preparation, technique, taste, and presentation—all must come together to meet or exceed the expectations of the guest. The only acceptable departure from the norm is to do it even better than the last time. This way, people will return to your table just as they might reread *Madame Bovary* or return for a second or third viewing of *The Godfather:* each re-experience reveals new pleasures.

Because you are consistent, your patrons may trust you to try something completely new. If you like the braised shortribs we serve at Café Boulud and you've always loved the sea bass, then you will probably give me the benefit of the doubt when I present Skate Wing Stuffed with Chanterelles Duxelles with Sauce Bordelaise.

I always look carefully at how a young chef self-manages in the one area where he has some latitude: his production and *mise en place*. Say we give you a bunch of leeks to julienne. You are only going to julienne the white parts. The young chef who will improve thinks ahead and asks, "What am I going to do with the greens?" They might be delicious for the staff meal. Or maybe you remember reading about Jean-Georges Vongerichten's lamb saddle dusted with black trumpet mushroom powder and a green leek purée, and you suggest something in that spirit. If you think like this you have an understanding that in haute cuisine we create a lot of waste, but there is always some way to use almost everything if you think about it long enough. Today, aiming to create no waste is so important that Dan Barber did a pop-up in London called wastED where he served a zero-waste menu.

One of the most memorable dishes I ever made grew out of this natural instinct to use everything and discard nothing, or almost nothing. It was back at the old DANIEL, before we moved from 76th to 65th Street in New York. Emeril Lagasse and the late Charlie Trotter, along with a half dozen friends, came for lunch. Now, one thing you need to know about chefs: we like to cook for each other, and we like to raise the bar with something that is really "out there." I had done a suckling-pig special two days earlier, so I had three heads sitting in the fridge ready to be given to one of the prep cooks to take home for pozole soup.

Then it occurred to me, why not give these superstar chefs something really primal, like a nice pig's head? I took a large copper sauté pan and meticulously lined it with apple-smoked bacon. Then I put the heads back to back and surrounded them with rustically cut apples, celery root, carrots, onions, lots of endive, rosemary, garlic, fresh cracked pepper, and salt. I pressed the vegetables tight against the pigs' heads then covered the whole thing with slices of bacon so that in effect you had a turban of bacon.

I roasted it for two and a half hours until the bacon was golden and crisp. When we presented the finished dish at the table, we cracked open the bacon crust, and the aroma erupted to fill the room with a smoky, unctuous perfume.

I believe Emeril's exact words were, "Yeah, man!"

Then we brought the heads back to the kitchen—the meat of the head was falling off the bone—and cracked the skull to eat the brains. We gave everybody at Emeril and Charlie's table a piece of ear, snout, jaw, some apple, endive, and the smoky-fatty *jus* from the bacon. This is how to make a chef happy when you feed him. Do not give him caviar; give him a pig's head. Needless to say, I do not have much call for bacon-wrapped suckling pig's head. In fact, that was the only time I ever made it. It was an unforgettable, spontaneous moment that I have yet to re-create, but this is the kind of thing chefs do for one another: pure whim, going with your gut, and having fun.

Which gets me back to a point that I cannot emphasize too many times: *do not waste anything.* Think instead of how you can fully utilize every ingredient or ensure that your leftovers are used smartly. The young chef who thinks ahead like this has an approach that takes in the total picture, both culinary and financial. Many chefs (including talented home chefs) can create wonderful recipes if they buy expensive ingredients, use them extravagantly, and waste all the trimmings and cooking liquids that inevitably result from any recipe. The true "chef in the raw" instinctively understands that waste is bad and increases food costs, so he or she figures out a way to use the totality of every product. When I see a young chef who thinks this way, it tells me that here is a person who not only understands food but also understands process and how to organize many things at once.

Do you remember how I told you that you must make yourself valuable to the chef? I am not only giving you good advice; I am doing a favor for whatever chef you work for as you begin your career. You see, everybody thinks that we top chefs are entertainers and magicians—that we personally have a hand in every dish that comes out of the kitchen. In fact, to believe this is to confuse the orchestra with the conductor.

Of course, true chefs pride themselves on their own cooking ability, but the truth is that as a chef gets more successful, he or she can no longer cook to the exclusion of everything else. That means carefully choosing the personnel with whom we chefs surround ourselves is critical.

If you become a top chef, being good is not good enough. You need to *hire* great. I remember an event I did in the late '80s at De Gustibus, the cooking school at Macy's, in which a young Asian man, Alex Lee, introduced himself. I was still at Le Cirque then, but I was thinking about striking out on my own. Alex and I made a great connection, but then he left New York to spend some time in France. He came back as the first chef de cuisine at DANIEL, and the two of us worked side by side, often seven days a week, for about ten years with a synergy I haven't had with anyone since. We could finish each other's sentences but also fueled each other's individual creativity and passion for the craft. It was a special era that I remember fondly. I have no doubt he's part of the reason DANIEL is what it is today.

So never worry that someone will come along who is as good as you are. Two good cooks—working as a team—are much more valuable than one good cook badly assisted. In cooking, as in music, harmony is greater than the sum of its parts. It opens up possibilities that are inaccessible to the solo chef. If you always work with good, dedicated people, both above and below you, then you will learn to thrive in an environment of excellence. At this stage of my career, I would not mind—indeed, I welcome—people working for me who can cook some things better than I can. Good people raise the whole level of the game. They also are in full charge of their programs at each restaurant. My people are my greatest asset, every one: the pot washer, the pastry cook, the waiters—they are all my allies. Treat them with respect, and they will remain an asset. Treat them as interchangeable and expendable, and you will have difficulty holding any team together. Turnover is inevitable, but earning loyalty among cooks is still the most rewarding accomplishment.

It is a fine and delicate balance, dependent on nuance and detail. Take the team on the road (which often happens when chefs do a guest appearance in another city or country) and the food is rarely as on the money as in the chef's home kitchen. After being in business for five years, I closed the original DANIEL (Café Boulud is there now) and relocated to the original home of Le Cirque, where I had cooked for so many years. I took my pots and pans, my recipes, and most of my staff and marched eleven blocks downtown to a new kitchen—seemingly not a very big move. But re-creating all those almost instinctual moves in an unfamiliar situation—new stove, new layout, having to reach to the right for a plate rather than the left, the rotisserie station being five steps from the meat line rather than three—affected timing, coordination, and, inevitably, the end result. We had to relearn to function as a team. We were good when we opened the new DANIEL, but not as smoothly efficient as we'd been at the old DANIEL. We were transplanted, and it takes time for any organism to accept a transplant. In the case of a restaurant, it takes time for even the best people to mesh in new surroundings and return to the top of their game.

When you work in a top restaurant, you naturally begin to feel some pride. This is good, but be careful. You need a healthy ego and driving ambition, but you also need to put them on the shelf for a while and concentrate on the needs of the chef for whom you are working. Young chefs *should* give two years to their mentor. Out of our hundred cooks, though, I have found that the ones who stay even longer and pay their dues succeed better than the impatient ones who move around to different places too fast.

I know about ego and ambition. I have a healthy dose of both. When I was a cook, I wanted to be a chef de partie. When I was chef de partie, I wanted to be a sous chef. When I was sous chef, I wanted to be chef. Then I wanted to be a restaurateur. Then I wanted to open another restaurant. It is inevitable, if you live and breathe this business, that your passion will grow, that this will fuel your ambition, and that your ego will help to drive it. These are all good things . . . in good time. But while you are a young chef, the motto in any respectable kitchen is: leave your ego at home, do your job the best you can, and soak up every lesson you can.

SOME ELEMENTS OF SUCCESS

WHEN YOU BECOME an executive chef, or chef-restaurateur, the first question you must ask yourself every day is, Why would people choose my restaurant? In a great city there are hundreds of choices, and we often share the same supplies, customers, and local business support. As a hip musician friend once asked, "Does it pass the 'Who cares' test?" In terms of what's trendy, dozens of restaurants serve pastrami-cured everything, grass-fed steaks, microherbs, burnt leeks, and so on. Or more classically, half a dozen places in New York shave as many truffles as we do and offer the best squab or the finest caviar.

So why would someone pick my place . . . or yours?

At the level of restaurant we are talking about, food is the first consideration, although comfort level (both emotional and physical) in the dining room also comes into play. That you have technique is taken for granted. That you serve the best ingredients is a given. It's not simply about ingredients. Nor, surprisingly, is it about perfection. It's a about a unique experience.

I do not mean this in some mystical sense (although a succulent leg of spring lamb can transport me into a state of nirvana). I mean it in the direct sense that the food has to give you a feeling of well-being. It needs to make you happy. Yes, the technique must be perfect—meticulous and precise. Yes, the food must amaze you. But first and last it must make you happy.

There are chefs who accomplish this through a daring and complex combination of ingredients and techniques, others through restrain and simplicity. Complexity is rewarding and even remarkable, but when the result, as in many cases, is simply a short-lived display of culinary fireworks, it can leave you amazed but not touched. As a chef, you want to move your patrons, to touch them with the honesty and personality in your food, service, decor, wine.

It all comes down to balance on the part of the chef. I constantly think of the creative tension between eccentricity and simplicity. The former without the latter leads to a grand fireworks display, but no oomph. Light but no heat. That is why I think simplicity is so important.

Jean and Pierre Troisgros put it very wisely when I was a young chef. They spoke of *La Règle de Trois,* or the Rule of Three. By this they meant that there should only be three main components in a dish. For example, their iconic dish, Saumon à l'Oseille, was composed of just wild salmon, white wine cream sauce, and sorrel. A delicate oceanic flavor tempered by the smooth creaminess of the wine sauce and the tanginess of the sorrel. Another inspiration, purely Lyonnais, is the combination of frog legs in a watercress velouté alongside wild mushrooms. My first chef at DB Bistro Moderne, Jean-François Bruel, dreamed it up using a classic combination of ingredients from my home region in a creative way. In 2003, Jean-François became the executive chef at Restaurant DANIEL, and once in a while he makes the same simple preparation with perhaps a touch more refinement, yet his history with the dish has made it somewhat of a new classic. Simple? Yes. But also inspired.

Or take one of my all-time signature dishes, the Paupiette of Sea Bass. I have probably sold more orders of this item in my career than anything else. It's very simple: sea bass in a crust of thin potato slices, served on a bed of leeks with a pungent, highly concentrated red wine sauce. I think part of the reason it became a classic in my repertoire, of course, has to do with its pleasing combination of tastes and textures, but equally so, its simplicity makes it something that lingers in your taste memory and never really goes out of style.

I am reminded of a meal I had when I took my sommelier to France to spend time with some of the great winemakers of Burgundy and the Rhône valley. It was a real party:

six good friends drinking great wine, eating great food. My longtime pal Dean Santon, the master of mixtapes, made us an entire trip's worth of traveling music: Howlin' Wolf, Django Reinhardt, the Clash, Bob Dylan. We had a big black BMW. I called this journey the 100,000 Calorie Tour because we ate more great food more often than you would think possible. In fact, some of the guys were convinced it was impossible, but when amazing food is on the agenda, somehow my capacity is hardly ever reached. As for wine, some days the tastings went from nine in the morning to seven at night. Even if you just look at that many wine bottles in a day, you get a buzz.

Making our way slowly to Burgundy, we stopped off at Georges Blanc in Vonnas. The place had grown since I'd worked there nearly thirty years before. Such an elegant but unfussy establishment. The wine room in the back of the restaurant was beautifully lit, and just to separate the true gourmets from casual foodies, Georges had one small shelf filled with bottles of *eau de vipère*—a French farmhouse tradition. Whenever a poisonous snake was found in a barn or around the house, farm families (including mine) would capture the snake, stick it in a wine bottle, fill the bottle with eau de vie, and let it sit for a few years. Because of the curve of the bottle, which acts like a big magnifying glass, you see a giant snake head. Georges had about twenty well-pickled vipers lined up on that shelf, and the display always got *ooh la la's,* especially from the ladies and children.

Georges made us a lovely tasting menu, and months later, when someone asked me to name the most memorable dish we had on our trip, it was not the amazing turbot en croûte from l'Espérance, or the rich and bold veal *en cocotte* with carrots and orange juice from Bernard Loiseau at La Côte d'Or, or the equally dazzling partridge and porcinis at Lameloise. What I remembered most was an exceedingly simple Georges Blanc vichyssoise with scallops, oysters, and caviar—in other words, a basic peasant dish, vichyssoise, transformed by a few pristine ingredients into something noble and sublime. Simplicity and glamour made it memorable.

Such a dish is eccentric, yes, but not so eccentric that it leaves people scratching their heads. Remember, if you are successful in establishing an identity, people will have certain expectations of you. If you have concentrated on a certain culinary tradition, then your eccentric dishes cannot be terribly far afield.

Cities such as Paris, London, New York, and San Francisco have a tremendous variety of ethnic communities whose heritage is often reflected in restaurants located outside their ethnic enclaves. I urge you to try as many of them as you can while you are starting out. It will pay off in the future when you are seeking inspiration. It is only through real experience—and lots of it—that you become well-versed in different culinary traditions and can begin to offer them to your clientele and, in so doing, differentiate yourself.

I am very clearly a product of the French culinary heritage. It has the longevity and depth to make it a resource of tradition as well as a source of evolution and creativity. Italian cuisine fits this bill too.

In Mexico City and New York, Enrique Olvera combines Mexican cuisine and modern technique at Pujol and Cosme. Rick Bayless has been mining this vein with great success for decades. In Portland, Oregon, Andy Ricker opened the first Pok Pok, a study in Thai cuisine. In San Francisco, Danny Bowien personalized Chinese food with many other influences. In Buenos Aires, the Argentinian Tomas Kalika has somehow managed to assimilate Eastern European, Sephardic, and Mizrahi food into an authentic remix of these disparate Jewish culinary traditions. In all these cases, you will note that the chef's innovations remain within a tradition. I have personally always been most secure within the European tradition, but if you choose some other cuisine, first make sure that it awakens a passion in you, second, make sure that you know it well, and equally important, make sure that there is a market for it.

The thing you want to avoid above all is a crazy eclecticism. So you walk the line between innovation and tradition.

You need the innovation, the eccentricity, to keep yourself interested and engaged. That is how I came up with a dish that I would call eccentric but also simple and direct. I always enjoyed eating sushi after work with the team or with friends at a convenient place that was open until three a.m. Beautiful Japanese mackerel. Toro as tender and pink as milk-fed veal. Hand rolls with spicy scallop and crispy oyster and superb uni. I rarely got out of there for less than $150. I would eat for hours, and I would not feel stuffed.

After years of eating there, I traveled in South America, where I became more familiar with ceviche. Given my love of these two raw cuisines, I felt confident that I should create something in the raw-seafood vein that would be true to my "inner chef." The result—part Daniel, part Japanese, part Peruvian—was a Chincoteague oyster filled with slices of live scallop, Osetra caviar, a sprinkle of lime and zest, oyster liquor, grated horseradish, and a garnish of crunchy celery, radishes, minced chives, and a spoonful of uni. A simple dish, all about balance and composition, but mostly it is about the purity and freshness of the sea, slightly briny with notes of the aromatic sharpness of iodine. Key to the concept of this dish is that the ingredients are so fresh that they impart a delicate, almost fragile quality to the completed recipe.

Where did that dish come from? From the love of sashimi, the oysters of my childhood, and the ceviche bars of Lima.

And from a certain hunger that goes off in a chef when you have assimilated tastes and techniques to the extent that a dish—or at least the idea for it—comes to you the way that daydreams do. All of a sudden, it is just there.

Creativity and innovation are forced upon you if you have a market-driven menu meeting the expectations of a knowledgeable and novelty-seeking clientele. When you are in tune with the markets and the seasons, you will come up with new dishes constantly. This is also where the whole team comes into play. For as long as I have been in the kitchen, collaboration has been one of the most exciting aspects of working with other people. It provides a daily dose of unfettered freedom of expression.

As a chef, you must have the confidence in yourself and your team that allows you to be open to the ideas of the other chefs. Believe me, they are full of ideas and excited for the chance to express them. New dishes or specials may come from a group of them or may start with one person's idea and get discussed around the kitchen until finally there is something worthy of your dining room.

Go with the flow. Also, go slow. New dishes evolve, and they gain complexity as they do. They need new techniques, or at least new combinations of techniques, and most of all, their own unique balance of tastes. I do not have all the answers in my repertoire. We learn as a group. True, I give advice and direction, but my chef de cuisine or sous chef will have the main task of working it out and may know something new about an ingredient or a method that we will all share. The great lesson in all this is that new recipes are never written in stone. They evolve every day until you reach the perfect balance.

You may not even be the one on your team who makes the correction that completes a dish. You may take it 90 percent of the way, but then someone will add 5 percent and someone else will add 2 percent or 3 percent until an almost good enough dish becomes something new and exciting. Feedback from the front of the house is always helpful. Finally, when you have a new recipe exactly how you want it, then you do write it in stone. Turn your creativity to the next new dish.

Innovation and creation are what keep this job interesting. Of course, you must know how to make a perfect coq au vin, but if all you do is turn out culinary photocopies of the classic dishes, in time you will become bored, and even the classics will lose some of their gusto. Failed recipes are never the problem. Failing to maintain or re-create them is.

THE FRONT OF THE HOUSE

You MAY BECOME a marvelous chef, the inventor of a whole new cuisine. You may have social media ramping up over your cooking—but if the people in your restaurant who interact with the public are not on their game, it really does not matter. Your customers only *think* they come to a restaurant merely for the food. What they really come for is more complex than that. Sure, they want a good meal, but they also want a pleasant time, nice surroundings, and a staff that treats them as if service is a pleasure.

A great front of the house with just okay food is likely to be more successful than a restaurant with mind-blowing food and surly waiters and maître d's. Everyone pays lip service to great service, but in the day-to-day crush of getting the meals cooked and served, it is easy to lose sight of what is going on outside the kitchen, beyond those double doors, where the check gets paid.

Do not ever lose sight of this. Every time you do, it will come back to bite you. If you really want to learn what service is all about, the best teacher—as in everything—is experience. When I was an apprentice in the kitchen in Lyon, I also worked as a server at the brasserie next door (on my day off). They were short one waiter, so I offered to help the owner. I figured he could use the extra hand, and by the same token I knew I could stand to learn a bit more about service. There was then (and to some extent, still is) a natural tension between waitstaff and kitchen staff. The front of the house is often thought of as more cheesy and superficial, with a tendency to put on airs. The kitchen often likes to think of itself as more artistic and pulling off more substance.

I quickly came to appreciate the mix of personality traits that go into the makeup of a good server: in a fine-dining restaurant you need to be intelligent, often multilingual, confident, and yet at the same time humble. I may have been smart for a young cook, but I was not a very good waiter. Still, it was a valuable experience. Up close and firsthand I saw that there are customers who are in a hurry, customers who change their minds, customers who "distinctly remember" asking for something other than what you serve them. There are chatty people, courteous people, and people who would not be pleased if Escoffier himself cooked the meal and served it on Napoleon's personal plates.

The front of the house has to deal with all these types, and though it is a test of your composure, you must treat each of them with the same care. That is what being a professional means. Being courteous to a charming customer is easy; being nice to a pain in the ass is professional.

The job of the restaurateur is, regardless of the situation, to make people feel comfortable. In some cases, the inherent dynamics of the restaurant as a scene of social interaction work decidedly against you. I am thinking in particular of the customer who has a chip on his or her shoulder no matter what you do. Your being nice may not change things very much. Part of the explanation for the natural combativeness of some diners is that we live in a world where things don't always go your way: Bad day at the office? Got blamed for something you didn't do? You can always take it out on the waiter.

That the waitstaff has done nothing or very little to deserve this treatment is beside the point. The customer lets it out simply because he or she can. It is human nature. The anger has to go somewhere, and the restaurant's failure to get the order exactly right or exactly on time is reason enough to dredge up the day's stored resentments.

Do not take this personally but rather as a challenge. Remember, in this business we use one word for the whole ensemble of activities, from cloakroom to kitchen to dining room, that make up the restaurant experience. That word is *service.* Your job is to serve, politely, professionally, and sincerely. The little things that make people feel special—from a smile at the door to a well-considered wine recommendation—can mean so much. Bear in mind that in a well-run restaurant, the unhappy and unsatisfiable represent a very small percentage; still, if not dealt with, they can ruin the night for you and your staff.

Never, *ever* argue with a customer. Never allow your staff to do so either. Once, I had a maître d' who came with very good references from some terrific New York restaurants. He also had miles of attitude. One day I saw him arguing with a customer. About forty-five seconds later he became my former maître d'.

Complaints, by the way, are not always unfounded. They are right as often as they are wrong, and they are invaluable. With a famous restaurant, almost everyone will tell you how great your food is and how great your place is. That is nice, but it does not necessarily help you improve. Not to mention that not all compliments are genuine.

Criticism, on the other hand, helps you make corrections. Teach your staff to be attentive and appropriately responsive to criticism. It's an opportunity to make improvements immediately. Some customers will be very direct when they are not happy and will let you know it. Others may feel unsure or at least uncomfortable in voicing displeasure, but they too communicate through body language and loss of enthusiasm. A good server will take cues from this and work to turn the experience around. The staff must have their antennae up. Often they can sense dissatisfaction in the dining room and address it before it gets to you.

An unhappy guest often communicates today through social media: posting reviews, photos, and one-liners, or even writing a letter to food critics and food guides. In this situation, unfortunately, you may not know there was a problem until it's too late. It is worth your time to pay attention to such posts. That doesn't mean you need to be checking in every five minutes and certainly never during service. You might even leave the task to one of your staff, but there is a whole lot of feedback out there, some of it as good as what can be given by the best focus group. And by all means, resist the temptation to reply in kind to nasty, snarky comments. It accomplishes nothing and makes you look as small as your detractors.

Although some diners come for a transcendental once-in-a-lifetime experience, some of our most loyal regulars come just as much for consistency and familiarity. Our waitstaff quickly learns that these diners do not want to be dazzled by some new invention every night. They want their favorite cocktail, a specific wine, and the food they love. The challenge is to lead these diners past their old favorites to new dishes. This can be a help to the kitchen because these members of our dining family often will be more frank in helping critique a new dish.

You might also consider doing as we do and hiring completely anonymous reviewers to come to your restaurant incognito and deliver a thorough eight-page critique of a typical three-hour dining experience: from making the reservation, to describing how long it took to get a martini, to the attentiveness of the waitstaff, and, of course, to the cuisine. It is money well spent.

Problems, though, are unavoidable. Sometimes, a situation can start in the lounge with a delay in seating and can get carried over to the meal. The server in the dining room needs to know that the customer has been made to wait, and he or she should make the kitchen aware of the need to be super prompt. When we have potentially displeased customers, the waitstaff is fully responsible for steering the guest toward a feeling of trust. Essentially, we have a brief time with the guest, and by the end of the meal the guest has to be very happy. Period.

If, on rare occasions, we get a letter of complaint, we know who the server was, who the assistant was, and what was ordered. We figure out what went wrong and how to avoid the same mistake happening again. In this we are helped by our logbook, in which the head of each department records what happened that evening, from a waiter's having run too fast in the dining room to the bread server cutting the bread too thick to a customer expressing dissatisfaction with a wine. The pluses and minuses in that logbook become the agenda for the next day's preservice meeting, in which we revisit every issue and figure out how to do better.

Sometimes a problem is nobody's fault. It is just the nature of the business. We try to predict in advance how the evening is going to play out. People arrive late. They cancel. Their reservation for seven becomes a reservation for three (or vice versa). Tending to 150 people in a restaurant over the course of an evening is different from entertaining 150 people in a theater. In the theater, the performance goes on whether 20 or 220 people show up, or a full house. In a restaurant, the "performance" is constantly in flux, and the whole evening is a series of separate performances, in a manner of speaking: each diner reacting to the particular way he or she is treated and whether the chef meets, exceeds, or falls short of expectations. The only thing you can be sure of is that a lot of curveballs will be thrown at you, and you just deal with them until the evening is through. A well-organized kitchen with a professional crew will alleviate issues.

If you are owner and chef, as I am, you may very well find yourself making a round in the dining room during service. I think this is a great idea, but it is not for every chef. Joël Robuchon, for example, rarely came out, but he was acknowledged as the top chef in Paris. Do it if you are comfortable, but be sure you are genuine.

Personally, I really enjoy working with the front-of-house team. Sometimes, when things are busy and the waitstaff is backed up, I will take an order or help serve something table-side. The staff appreciates it. The customers appreciate it. I just love pretending that I could be a waiter too. I often tell my team that to be a great professional in service you have to have "the eye of the falcon"—meaning you should be able to survey the room at all times and see from any distance if the guests miss or need something. You must always read the moves and mood of the guest. Anticipation is key, but it requires great focus, a real sense of hospitality, and a passion for service.

Bottom line: do whatever it takes to make service go seamlessly and keep everybody happy. You will be greatly rewarded if you have at least one talented professional in the dining room management who can teach someone the skills of making people feel at ease, of being attentive without being overbearing. Your staff should be generous and friendly with your guests while always staying within the boundaries of professionalism. They may forge relationships, friendships even, but they must remember they are the server to the guest.

The line between warm and hospitable versus casual and too friendly with guests is a thin one, but it must be maintained.

I had the privilege to work with someone who mastered this nuance with grace and decorum. In the thirty years I worked with him, he had my great admiration and respect. Bernard Vrod and I first met in 1986, when I started as the chef at Le Cirque, and we celebrated his retirement (along with that of his wife, Ginette, who was our faithful *gouvernante*) in early 2016. His sister Cecile, son Yannick, and brother-in-law Giovanni have all worked at DANIEL over the years, and many of our regulars still associate Bernard with the restaurant. He had an incomparable ability to recall guests' preferences, their dislikes, and their children's names alike. He could charm a table with his personality, all the while respecting the guests' privacy and the formality of the situation. Throughout his career he served seven US presidents, many foreign dignitaries, and countless famous actors and artists, but more important, if he was your server at DANIEL, he treated you the same way as he treated them: like royalty. And he did it for thirty years without ever becoming jaded. He worked with joy and pride in the service of others and always inspired the young waiters with his knowledge and experience.

It is human nature to create a personal relationship with your best customers. After all, they have made the investment in you. Recently, I had a customer who had spent thousands of dollars on wine with us. At the end of one of my tasting menus, he said, "Wonderful, exquisite, but I would love some tripe."

So the next week, when he came back, I made tripe for him as a surprise, a very basic peasant dish, but dolled up with chorizo, black olives, cranberry beans, calf's feet, tomato confit, and a buttery crust of sourdough bread. He was beyond himself, beaming with joy.

I hope you will always listen to your customers and try to meet their wishes. It is the same in every great place, from roadside diner to Michelin-starred restaurant.

A SPECIAL KIND OF LIFE

———◆———

ONE THING THAT becomes apparent to you very quickly is that when the rest of the world is having fun, you are working. Saturday night, you work; Christmas, you work; Easter, Fourth of July, Mother's Day, Thanksgiving . . . ditto. If you want to be a chef, you cannot compare your life to others'. The chef's world is a different world. The hours are longer, the work more intense than in many other walks of life. But you really do not dwell on it. At least I never did.

Sure, I would love to go to more movies, go out with my friends more, spend more time at home, but I made a choice when I was fourteen and I never looked back. Restaurants are my passion and they consume me. If anything, as time goes by, restaurant life becomes more consuming. As perfection becomes more attainable, it also becomes more and more the center of your life. Where other passions may cool with time, the chef's gets hotter.

Anyone who can find this kind of guiding passion in life is very lucky, because so many people never experience the sense of mission and maturing skill that a chef's career brings. From your first day, you must seek out the best mentors, the best restaurants, the best suppliers, and the best partners as you go through this career, because you are only as good as the background you acquire and the people with whom you work.

I do not mean to suggest that being a chef requires self-denial, as though you were some medieval monk. The restaurant kitchen—sensual, raucous, and intense—becomes its own world. You may not get to hang out with friends much outside work, but you will develop deep friendships in the kitchen. And you will be doing the thing you love the most and building a global network of friends who share the same passion.

In the end, doing what you love is what matters and will make you a better chef. The sacrifices, even the successes, are add-ons. The heart of the matter is that you are doing what you love. As time passes, your ambition will carry you from one milestone to another: from mastering a recipe to opening your own restaurant. The further you go, the more you will be controlled by your craft and ambition to become better and sometimes bigger, to open more places, to do more. At a certain point, achieving success is no longer a distant goal. At that point, taking control of your success and balancing it with being a parent, spouse, and friend take center stage.

As it is with a good recipe, combining these ingredients for living can be endlessly fine-tuned, reworked, reinvented; for each of us, the formula is different. As for working out that recipe . . . well, I cannot tell you the measurements, but I hope I have been able to get you motivated to start. Remember: as a young chef, cook with passion and emotion, do it with devotion, and defend your reputation. With that, someday you will be the new leader in the business.

Now, go cook! And maybe one day I will be reading your book.

THE TEN COMMANDMENTS
OF A CHEF

———◆———

1. Keep your knives sharp and take care of your tools
Your knife is your most essential tool. A sharp knife makes
a big difference in the precision and consistency of your
knife work, and if it does not perform, it means you have not
taken care of it. Having the *right* knife for the job is just as
important. Both the quality and upkeep of your tools bear a
significant impact on your work, so make sure they are top
priorities. In the modern toolbox, you may have knives from
different countries—Germany, France, Japan, Switzerland,
even hand-crafted knives from America—but keep in mind
that the latest, most expensive Japanese blade is not the only
solution. I have a number of old French knives that are work-
horses, and they suit me just fine. Like a craftsman, you get
attached to your tools and learn the purpose of each one.

2. Work with the best people

To become a great chef you do not need to work with twenty top chefs. You need to experience working with three or four very good chefs. The best is not necessarily the most popular or most famous; it can just as easily be a chef in a small place who is simply very organized and very good. Focus on a few chefs for your foundation, then for specialties—for example, charcuterie, pastry, and so on—you can do internships. Today I'm as committed as ever to mentoring and connecting with the young chefs in my restaurants, so I'm more interested in the cook who has moved up the ranks in a respectable albeit lesser-known establishment than the cook who has jumped around the best kitchens, often taking away more than he gave, all toward an end goal of stacking his résumé with big names. Find a mentor and develop a relationship, then work hard to guarantee that he/she writes you a personal recommendation for your next job. I receive countless references, and the ones that are heartfelt mean so much more than a paper pedigree.

3. Keep your station orderly

From the storage of vegetables to the finishing of *mise en place,* everything needs to be marked, labeled, and placed in the proper containers, taking up the minimum of room. Then, during service, you will not find yourself drowning in incoming orders. Instead, you will be able to focus on cooking well and sending clean plates with maximum efficiency. A clean space yields a clear mind, which yields fast hands and smart decisions. A well-organized station also gets respect from the rest of the kitchen.

4. Waste not!

Nothing is a greater sin than taking a round vegetable, making it into a rectangle, and throwing the rest out. Every ingredient has a price tag, and you have both a moral and an economic obligation to transform it fully into delicious food. Waste is the mark of a chef with a lack of imagination in recycling and a lack of dedication to his financials. Chefs must also pay attention to the prices of ingredients and keep them in line with what a customer will pay for a dish. Cooking has a lot to do with mathematics, and chefs must think carefully about ratios and making the right proportion of *mise en place*. The more you utilize everything, the more you will be able to afford the best ingredients. Still, a great chef respects the culinary value of every ingredient—from truffle to turnip.

5. Season with precision

The taste of every ingredient is elevated by proper seasoning. There is an exact point at which ingredients are seasoned correctly. Too much is too much, too little is too little, and somewhere in between is just right. Learning the peculiarities of your palate and attuning it to finished results requires precision and endless practice. It also requires constant tasting and self-critique. With time and experience you will gain confidence and will learn to naturally trust the process.

6. Master the heat

From 120°F to 800°F, there is an enormous range within which heat can transform ingredients, but the range is even greater when you factor in the types of heat: dry, steam, induction, convection. A truly great cook has such an intimate knowledge of heat that he or she develops a sixth sense of timing for the moment of doneness. You might rarely have the opportunity, but the most exciting and challenging is to cook over fire; it requires skill, instinct, and constant adjustment to yield a great result. Learn the basics of heat and then pay close attention to the nuances so that you can cook confidently, no matter the ingredient or the method.

7. Learn the world of food

Experience different cuisines whenever you can. Do it when you are young, before you are building your career. Learning other cuisines will broaden your foundation as a chef. Today, globalization is a forgone conclusion, and although it's easier than ever to be exposed to other cuisines, what is considered "basic food knowledge" is more substantial than it used to be. Many things that were once obscure and exotic are ubiquitous today. Still, the Internet is no substitute for tasting and seeing with your own eyes, so use your time off to go places, try new restaurants, buy books, talk to people. In other words, immerse yourself in the world of food. When you grow as a chef, having such broad knowledge will help you to hone in on the cuisine you like the best. Not every dish should feature elements from around the world; finding focus is just as important.

8. Know the classics

No matter what cuisine you concentrate on, the classic dishes will cover the spectrum of techniques and ingredients needed to master cooking. The fundamentals of stocks, sauces, and seasoning are all there in the classics . . . whether the classic is clam chowder in Cape Cod or bouillabaisse in Marseilles. Knowing the classics also gives you an edge in the kitchen. When the chef says to make a dish à la Clamart, a well-studied cook knows to garnish it with peas. Many dishes are classically or regionally coded this way. In the beginning it may feel like learning an entirely new language (namely, French), but in professional kitchens that language is universal, and being fluent will get you far. It also signals to the chef that you respect tradition and the institution.

9. Accept criticism and push yourself

As a young chef, you spend your days and nights being criticized and analyzed by the chefs for whom you work. It is important to learn from criticism. It is equally important to learn how to criticize usefully when you become a full-fledged chef. And finally, you must learn from the criticism of the public. Recognize that to keep yourself interested you are constantly varying, innovating, and reinventing, succeeding at times and needing more work at others. Criticism is the public's way of telling you how to improve on the results of your creative impulses. You must understand that to earn accolades, you have to go beyond your duties and assist and care for everything in the kitchen. Be prepared: criticism will come often; praise will be hard-earned.

10. Keep a journal of your recipes

You cannot remember everything you see cooked, or even everything you've cooked yourself, but with a journal, a computer, and the camera on your phone, you can bring those taste memories to life to guide you for the rest of your career. Even with today's technology, however, I often still jot recipes, notes, and ideas by hand. Many find they are more likely to retain information by writing it. I have always tended toward drawing out my ideas, because for me, sketching stimulates creativity, but it also helps me to see the full picture and explain the thought. In our kitchen, the cooks always have a small notebook so they can record the elements of a dish or recipe and refer to it later. Snapping a photo of a recipe may be quick and helpful in the moment, but it's unlikely you will process and commit it to memory the same way. A journal is a great tool for a disciplined cook.

A FEW LETTERS FROM MY FRIENDS

DISCIPLINE

◆

by Gavin Kaysen

I'VE ALWAYS SAID that the eight years I spent working for Daniel Boulud as executive chef at Café Boulud was like getting my PhD in hospitality and cooking. When I started, I already had a solid foundation—I was a good chef, and I'd had a pretty well-rounded culinary education. But Daniel was at another level. When it came to hospitality, Chef would notice if the street outside was too noisy, if the room was too bright, or if the phones weren't answered on the first ring; he was always genuinely concerned with the guests' comfort. In terms of cooking, he taught me the classics: how to make food "tell a story," and how to make simple food elegant and delicious.

If there was one thing that prepared me the most for this sort of higher education, it was discipline. Luckily, discipline has always been a part of me. Maybe it was how I grew up or maybe it's innate, but in Daniel's kitchen it was a way of life, and I came to embrace it as a tool for perfection. Discipline can be a strong word, but it doesn't mean you have to be cold and militaristic. For me, discipline is about having a sense of routine, order, and control. Discipline is doing things the right way, even when circumstances vary, and even when you may not feel up to it.

In my first six months at Café Boulud, I won the James Beard Foundation's Rising Star Chef award—a great honor—and I was totally shocked. The evening was thrilling, and at the end of the night I called Daniel, who was out of town, working. We spoke about the awards ceremony and the evening in general, and he asked where I was going to party and celebrate, so I told him. At the end of the conversation he said something that I have never forgotten: "Don't be late for work tomorrow." I am still not sure if he said it jokingly, but I got home at six a.m., slept for three hours, and then went to work at ten a.m., like I was scheduled to do. Even if he was kidding, I knew that was the sort of discipline he expected from me.

There was a point when I first started to work for Daniel that I thought, *I've really come far.* But it was quickly clear to me that I was back to being a student. Although I was at the helm of a French restaurant, I learned that what I thought about French cuisine was only what was in my mind, and I needed to immerse myself in every cookbook I could get my hands on. I became addicted to what it meant to be French:

how they ate, how they cooked, how they relaxed. I thought if I could learn those traits, I could cook better for my French chef. I realized that running a French kitchen was about instilling in the team the values of tradition, respect (both for the ingredients and for oneself), and, of course, discipline.

I wanted to inspire cooks the way Daniel inspired me. I remember reading the first edition of *Letters to a Young Chef* when I was twenty-six years old and living in San Diego, California. I felt an immediate connection to the words, ideas, and advice. I knew I had to work for him; there was no way around it. So I formed a plan and started down a path, and I made critical choices that changed my life forever. Having the discipline to follow through with those choices and push forward down that path is what made it all a reality. Realizing your goals is not just about working for the best—it is about making you better so *you* can become the best.

Sometimes discipline requires you to push yourself to a level you have not experienced, to work with a proficiency that you didn't know you had in you. Then when you get there, you see if you can push further. Every time you have to do that task, you get better, always working your muscles, making them stronger and faster, going harder than the person next to you. You are pushing for something that may be unreachable, but you will achieve it simply because you are that driven, that good, and because you have the discipline to work at it.

Having success at Café Boulud was extremely fulfilling. However, Daniel was always one or two steps ahead of me. I can remember many times when we traveled together, across the country and even abroad. It was a lot of work, involving long, jam-packed days. Once we returned to New York, the driver would pick us up at the airport and take us back to Restaurant DANIEL. Daniel would go into work to greet the guests, say hello to the team, and finish the service, while I would go home to see my wife and catch up on sleep. Every time I felt the urge to pat myself on the back, I would look at him, and he'd be running circles around me.

There will be days that are difficult, when things do not go well or are harder than they should be. That's just life. But for me, on those days especially, following a sense of order and pushing to do things right are what get me through. Working with good habits must always stay a priority, because on some days that is all you have. When it feels like the rush of service is getting the best of you, and things just are not working out, stop, wipe down your station, give your tools a good rinse, and jump right back in.

Today, at my restaurant, Spoon and Stable, those lessons from Daniel are at play in everything I do, and I have worked to pass along those skills to my team. From our relationships with our purveyors to the way we set up for service— even to how we organize the walk-in—it all comes down to discipline. Beyond that, it is just as important to stay curious, cook with passion, and be hospitable to every guest, employee, farmer, and vendor. Of course, the most important thing I learned from Daniel is to stay true to who you are, through all the noise.

TECHNIQUE

---

by Jean-François Bruel and Eddy Leroux

GOOD TECHNIQUE IS probably the most underrated aspect of professional cooking in America today, and it has never been the most glamorous. Really good technique requires a level of patience and discipline that many prefer to bypass in exchange for the adrenaline rush of shuffling pans during service or complicated ingredient manipulation and technology. Tasks like carefully washing mushrooms, tying a roast, or cutting a perfect *brunoise* too often come in second to the more interesting elements of being a chef, such as creating dishes or working with rare and expensive ingredients. This is a mistake, but as a young chef you still have time to fix it.

Technique is the foundation of everything you will ever do in the kitchen, so it should be important to you from the very start, but don't rush the process. Investing your time in learning correct technique is like learning basic grammar in a new language: you have to go through the tediousness of memorizing nouns and verbs before you can delve into an interesting conversation. With food, basic techniques have been codified because they actually enhance the flavor and make a better end result. It takes time to develop the muscle memory required to master certain knife skills, and it takes a constant curiosity about the science behind certain recipes in order to really know them intimately, to the point where you can make something perfectly without thinking too hard about it. This proficiency only comes after repetition and practice. And then even more practice. Eventually, good technique becomes second nature.

Take a basic béarnaise, for example. You all learn it as a young cook, but you may need to make it a hundred times to really master it. In the beginning it takes concentration to avoid overcooking the egg yolk. Then, still managing the temperature, you add your warm clarified butter at just the right tempo. You might screw it up twenty-five times out of a hundred, but eventually you do it perfectly every time because your technique is good and you have practiced—a lot. This is the ultimate goal: knowing a process so intimately that you can do it without stress or self-doubt.

Good technique is not just about prep, sauces, and knife cuts, however. It can also refer to steps or actions you take that elevate the outcome of a recipe from good to great to excellent, like correctly buttering a soufflé ramekin, which will ensure a smooth rise and beautiful result. This technique applies to every flavor of soufflé imaginable—even savory. At DANIEL, we make a lobster mousseline that follows a similar formula. We prepare small stainless-steel ramekins by brushing the tempered butter from the bottom to the top, chilling them, then applying another coat the same way. If we don't do it properly, the recipe fails. The same can be said for piping choux batter or building a complex terrine. The overall achievements, in both beauty and flavor, are earned in the detailed, technical know-how of the steps and also by knowing the end result before you start.

The good news is the more you strengthen your foundation, learning the basics, the more creative you can be. This is when cooking really gets fun. Borrowing techniques from other cuisines and applying them in interesting ways to your own cuisine can create a unique profile. But the classic ways of butchering meat and preparing vegetables are the support to this, and if they are not done properly, the creativity doesn't succeed. On the other hand, when everything is done right, it comes together in a way that can potentially bring great results. If you give ten cooks a raw chicken and a copper pot you will have ten different end results, but the one with impeccable technique is sure to cook the best one. Good technique allows you to put your great ideas into motion, so if creativity is something that motivates you, make sure to focus on technique for now.

Of course, you can learn many things online or from inexpensive used books that can be shipped to you overnight. You can be inspired by things you see cooked on TV, YouTube, Instagram, or Facebook. Back in the early '90s we mostly had books and the sternness of a good chef to motivate our education. Although you should take advantage of all the easily accessible resources you have, nothing can substitute for practice or the presence of a good chef to monitor and guide your development. For this reason, working in fine dining is still a crucial element of your training, even if is not where you ultimately want to plant your roots. It might seem more like boot camp, but doing so is the best source of new knowledge and inspiration. Today there are many good restaurants that have a more relaxed kitchen atmosphere, but the great ones achieve this without compromising on proper technique.

MENTORSHIP

by Barbara Lynch

MORE SO NOW than ever, mentorship is a key resource for the rising generation of young cooks. Our industry is growing so quickly that it seems we can somehow lose sight of where it all begins: with the basics. With the guidance of a mentor, the learning, understanding, and mastering of fundamental techniques provides the essential foundation needed to develop your own style as a chef. In the age of social media, when our work (and our lives!) is visible to so many people and when we in turn are exposed to so much, I urge you not to lose sight of your training as you develop a culinary vision. Do not let yourself be distracted by what might be trending on social platforms, or by what is currently perceived as "in." Without the solid support of basic skills, a young cook and his or her cuisine cannot withstand the strain of our industry or, ultimately, the test of time. A respect for classic technique and quality ingredients will never let you down.

It was not by sheer luck that Paul Bocuse earned three Michelin stars and has retained them since 1965—the longest of any three-star chef. As a young cook, he trained under three-Michelin-star chef Fernand Point, the father of modern French cuisine, who, while embracing the tenets of classic French cuisine, did not confine himself to them. So, too, Paul Bocuse built on what he learned under Fernand Point to make his own mark. He ultimately pushed the boundaries of traditional *cuisine classique* and ushered in a new culinary movement, nouvelle cuisine. The natural give-and-take between mentor and rising chef is what drives progress in the culture of kitchens worldwide. It simultaneously feeds our passion for cooking and facilitates the passing of vision from one generation of chefs to the next.

I've made it a priority to provide educational resources to my staff, both front and back of house. Together, we create an environment that fosters growth and upward mobility through teaching and mentorship. On all levels and across disciplines, we make ourselves better by learning from each other. Seek out a chef and a kitchen that will provide the same opportunity to you. And, when in doubt, returning to the basics will never steer you wrong. Once you know fundamental technique, your passion can drive you to achieve your dreams. I speak from experience when I say that if I could find success in this way, then you can too.

The one question I'm asked time and time again is, "What has been your biggest life lesson?" My answer remains the same: First of all, I'm still alive so I can't say for sure yet! But there is always more to learn. As long as I live, I'll continue to adapt, learn, and perfect.

My best piece of advice to you is do not underestimate the power of mastering basic, classic technique. Do this by passionately paying attention to the lessons from your mentor. From there, learn as much as you can from the others around you as a means for continued and lifelong improvement.

FLAVOR

————◆————

by Corey Lee

FOR A CHEF, everything is secondary to flavor. Sure, there are aspects of being a chef that are related to design, science, music, and other fields, but our primary role—unique to this profession—is to deliver great flavor.

Since the earliest days, home cooks have transformed ingredients to provide nourishment and calories. Yes, they, too, catered to tastes, but chefs made cooking a profession by dedicating themselves to the pursuit of greater flavor and in the process helped to develop regional cuisines and inspire their continued evolution. If your motivation to be a chef does not come from this core connection to flavor, then perhaps another profession is better suited to you.

I know all this sounds pretty obvious, but even as someone who has been at this for over twenty years, I only truly realized the importance of flavor later in my career. In the early years of my training, I wasn't working on menu development, and my tasks focused more on the mastery of a technique rather than the delivery of great flavor. When fluting mushrooms, for example, I'd concentrate on the angle of my hand movements or how much force to use—not necessarily on how it would end up tasting.

I took more pride in how quickly I finished my *mise en place* or how fast I worked a station, but I neglected to dwell on whether a guest might find my cooking delicious. In that sense, I was more of an athlete than a chef. Kitchens can be like machines of organization, training you to be technically proficient, quick, clean, consistent, and efficient. The lessons of flavor come at a much slower pace compared to those of organization and technical execution. And in the hierarchy of a traditional kitchen, working on flavor is the last responsibility, reserved for those at the top of the totem pole.

The trajectory of young cooks today appears to differ from that of my generation. Toiling away for years and years to learn the mechanics of cooking seems to no longer be the norm—a change that is both good and bad. It's great that cooks at such an early age seem to be more worldly and cerebral in how they view cuisine. But sometimes I worry that there's too much focus on form and concept at the outset. At a time when images and stories about food often take center stage, flavor is wont to take a back seat. It's easy to make food look beautiful or sound intriguing with seemingly disparate ingredients or *en vogue* menu descriptions. The mark of a skilled chef, however, is one who has met his purpose in creating great flavor, and no amount of visual embellishment or alluring introduction can help in this respect. It simply takes a lifetime of practice and learning.

In hindsight, I think I only started to come into my own as a chef once I truly realized the power of flavor and shifted my cooking to make that more of the focus. I now concern myself with compositions led by flavor and address presentation later. At Benu, I'm able to experiment with different ingredients and techniques—like those lent by Cantonese dried seafood or Korean lactic fermentations—and integrate them with my classical training to yield new flavors.

This has helped me evolve as a chef and connect with my native culture in a greater way. The latter was unplanned, but not surprising given that flavor is intrinsically linked to the identity of an area or culture or time. The ability to transcend taste and tap into something lasting makes flavor such a powerful tool. And for me, this is when our profession is most impactful and the potential of our work limitless.

One of the most exciting things about being a young chef is that you so have much to learn and discover. Reflecting on my own early years, here are some more practical pieces of advice:

Invest some years into working in one place. It's good to travel and stage, but being comfortable in a restaurant and getting past the natural learning curve that comes along with being in a new environment helps you get to a place mentally where you can really work and think about flavor. I worked for Thomas Keller at the French Laundry for nine years, which allowed me to delve into the repertoire or even a single dish, working on improving its flavor from one season to the next, from year to year. That kind of meticulous process requires commitment and discipline, but I think it's worthwhile for all young chefs at some point to commit years to a single kitchen.

If you work in a professional kitchen, the chances are you'll be tasked with making the family meal one day. Don't just brush it off as a side job that gets in the way of finishing your *mise en place.* I've never met a great chef who couldn't quickly whip up something delicious for the staff. One of my biggest pet peeves is seeing a cook with a fancy résumé who can't make a simple, tasty dish.

Cook at home, and eat the entire dish from start to finish. I've found in general that, whereas poor amateur cooks tend to underseason their food, poor professional cooks tend to overseason because they're only tasting a spoonful at a time. Eating what you cook and season in its entirety is a different experience and will help you understand how flavors build.

Try to explore the flavors of cuisines that are foreign to you. If there is a culture of people who enjoy a certain flavor profile, then there must be something to learn from the history and evolution of that cuisine.

When dining out, go beyond simply identifying the ingredients you taste, and ask yourself, "What was done differently to coax these kinds of flavors from the ingredients?" Understanding the variables in the cooking process that yield different flavors allows you to cook more intuitively.

Although food is universal, learning about flavors in an analytical way can transform the act of eating something familiar into a completely new experience. A fruit you've had a hundred times suddenly becomes another taste in your toolbox of flavors with the potential to inform your own cooking. Enjoy this time as a young chef! You're participating in a great tradition, and I look forward to tasting the even better flavors that the next generation creates.

INGREDIENTS

———◆———

by Eric Ripert

I STRONGLY BELIEVE that without quality ingredients, we can't have great cuisine. Even if you are a culinary genius, if you start with mediocre product, you will ultimately have a mediocre dish.

In French cuisine and Western cuisine in general, recipes are based mostly on fresh ingredients, whereas in some countries in Scandinavia and Asia, such as Korea, they use products that have been fermented. Even so, that process always begins with high-quality ingredients. Often, especially with game or meat, we mature them for weeks; however, once again, we use top-class products.

Cooking is artistic, a craftsmanship that I believe is a great exercise in mindfulness; therefore, nothing is more rewarding than to use the best and freshest ingredients of the moment. Nothing is more exciting than going to the market during the summer and smelling the basil, the sweetness of strawberries, fresh tomatoes at their peak, and so on. It's a great pleasure to cook with those ingredients at their best and to share them with an audience that is delighted by their qualities. You don't eat a tomato salad in January or coq au vin in August; it just doesn't sound (or taste) right. Ingredients at their best pay homage to the season and should be exalted during that time.

At Le Bernardin, we understand that seafood is very delicate and very perishable, so we dedicate all our efforts and passion to elevating the qualities and virtues of the fish. A few extra hours of mishandling and the product's flesh can be damaged and the quality reduced. We are very cautious with—and focused on the quality of—the seafood we receive. When we buy shellfish like oysters and clams, we make sure that they do not smell fishy, that they are clean and heavy, which means they are alive and full of juices. We make sure our lobsters are alive, and we always check to ensure that their bellies are very plump, full, and firm. We avoid lobsters that have a mushy or cotton-like consistency. When assessing our whole fish (the only way we purchase fish at Le Bernardin), we look for bright eyes and bright red gills, and we make sure that when we poke the fish, the flesh rebounds quickly. If the fish has scales, they should be dense and firmly attached to the skin. The final test is to open and smell the belly of the fish, which should never smell of low tide but of fresh ocean. In our loins of tuna, mostly yellowfin for sustainability reasons, we look for color—not brown, which means old or mishandled, and not too red, as that will impart a bloody flavor. A light ruby flesh is the best. Ultimately, the most important test for fresh seafood is, ironically, having no "fishy" smell. Another important factor for us is sustainability. We do not serve endangered species of fish, and we aim to support all efforts to preserve healthy stocks and respect the balance of the marine ecosystems.

Every great chef and cook I know searches for the freshest and highest-quality ingredients, and treats them with the utmost respect. Cooking doesn't start in the kitchen; it begins with growing, sourcing, and purchasing your ingredients before you begin to prepare them. Paying very close attention to each stage of the process ensures a better dish—and greater pleasure for your guests.

RECIPES

---

by Dominique Ansel

WILLY WONKA MAY have misled us all. The story of the chocolatier so protective over his recipes that he closed his factory and hired a team of Oompa Loompas who could not communicate beyond their native language taught the world one lesson: recipes were the key.

When you become a chef, you realize how wrong that assumption is. I first entered the kitchen at the age of sixteen, and at the time recipes were a highly guarded secret—kept in handwritten notebooks by the chef's side. The thought was that if you could only have the book of recipes, you would be able to open your own place and be the chef. Like a magician who didn't want to reveal his tricks, the chef would give only a portion of the recipe to each cook to prepare. Then, by himself, in secret, he would combine the results. The cooks peeked curiously over his shoulder and tried to see his motions through side glances across the kitchen. The final product was always a delight and a mystery. Maybe, just maybe, if you're good, the chef will let you know what actually went in there.

I don't know about you, but I thought that was a most ridiculous way to run a kitchen. It's not that I don't respect great and well-tested recipes. But I've always known that they were guidelines, not rules. Yes, you should absolutely try to scale things appropriately. And definitely don't take shortcuts or stray from each crucial step. But if you're a studious cook, like I was, and carefully make sure to do everything exactly as the recipe says, but still don't get the right result— well, like I said, recipes aren't everything.

Try baking the same mix in a different oven; you'll find that the cooking times can vary drastically. Use a different type of flour and butter; the results will never be the same. Even the weather can play a factor. In the wintertime, for instance, we often have to increase the yeast level in our doughs because the colder "room temperature" makes it difficult for the yeast to activate. I've even received a batch of eggs that had lower-than-normal protein levels, and so the egg whites wouldn't whip as well. A batch of ripe strawberries certainly calls for less sugar than sour ones. Cooking is a bit like predicting the weather. You can see a storm coming, but you have to adjust as you gauge exactly when it will arrive, and you must be ready for it to change at the last minute.

One of the greatest lessons I learned early in my career was that rather than finding out *what* goes into a recipe, it is far more important to understand *why*. It takes calibration. Think of a recipe as a guitar: it needs to be tuned before you can play a song. By knowing the effects that each ingredient has on the recipe, you'll be able to tweak the formula to one that yields the best results. And then one day you create your own.

People ask me all the time if, like Willy Wonka, I keep a stash of secret recipes somewhere. I laugh and point to an opened binder in the kitchen, where all our recipes are kept for easy access. We walk each of our cooks through the process in detail. "I don't believe in 'secret recipes,'" I reply. "Take the recipe away from Willy's hands, give it to a different chocolate factory, have a non–Oompa Loompa work on it— and I guarantee you would not have the same Wonka Bar."

CREATIVITY

by Grant Achatz

I LOVED BEING a chef de partie. I fed off the adrenaline of a busy night, the more impossible the better. I relished the pressure to be perfect with every cut, sear, and sauce. The repetitive nature of a professional kitchen encouraged me to become more intimately connected with the ingredients and to continually refine the preparation of each dish. What started as a desire to please the chef turned into a drive to challenge myself. Learning to intuitively "know" was my goal.

As much as I respected the discipline required to be a great cook, I was eventually drawn to the freedom and intensity of the creative process. Following ideas from conception to realization is incredibly satisfying, but devising my own ideas and then watching people interact with them, both in the kitchen and in the dining room, are even more rewarding. I am often asked why we continue to develop new dishes at Alinea since we have enough recipes to rotate through the seasons and makes guests happy. Why did we decide to demolish the restaurant and start over in 2016 after ten years of success? The answer is: if you removed my outlet for creativity, I would be left with just execution.

People like to think the creative process is romantic. The artist drifts to sleep at night, to be awakened by the subliminal echoes of his or her next brilliant idea. The truth, for me at least, is that creativity is primarily the result of hard work and study. The lightbulb goes off unexpectedly at times, a consequence of associating everything else I see, smell, hear, and touch with food. The sudden tempo change in a song suggests a dish that will achieve a similar shift in menu flow, breaking monotony in sequence or flavor profiles. The scent of a woman's perfume leads me to construct a dish based around the emotionally powerful aspect of smell.

What I realized over the years is that creativity is not an easy equation. And there is no direct line. You are not born with it, and you cannot learn it. It is a combination of dedication, practice, study, passion, and desire all coming together at one time. Those things are impossible to force; they must arrive in a perfect storm.

I am the most creative in the morning hours at the restaurant, after the last guest has departed, the chefs have handed out the orders for the next day and signed off, and the night cleaner has started tearing apart the stove. In the still silence of the dining room, with lights dimmed to a shadowy glow, I surround myself with my resources: a laptop, a notepad, pens, a glass of wine, a few reference books, a stack of C-fold paper towels with scribbled notes accumulated throughout the day, and a list of seasonal ingredients. When people ask me what my most important kitchen gadget is, I always respond, "The Internet." Google has been a huge resource for me over the years as a creative tool. Sourcing ingredients and researching different cuisines on the Internet became a huge well of inspiration. That was in 2002.

Now with Twitter and Instagram, chefs can instantly be inspired by each other from all over the world. We all have our phones on the pass, watching in real time what is happening in gastronomy. I can literally see what my colleagues are doing in New York, Tokyo, Lima, and Minneapolis.

Although technology and techniques are a focus at Alinea, the upcoming season and its corresponding inventory of ingredients guide me in developing a new menu. Of course, there are exceptions. If we are able to apply a new technique to an available ingredient, we will likely introduce a new dish as soon as it is developed. Excitement over the new can make us impatient. But more often, the list of ingredients defines the parameters within which I work. My approach to them comes down to an equation that is true of all cooking: ingredients plus manipulations equals finished dish. I remember a moment at the end of the summer in 2004 at Trio. As sous chef John Peters and I watched the last tomato dish leave the kitchen, I turned to him, shrugged, and said, "Great . . . what are we going to do next summer?" And so the thought process began, somewhere in the back of my mind: what ingredients, what manipulations, and how many permutations? The equation becomes more complicated, and usually takes a few wrong turns, before we find the answer. But it all boils down to the same logical process that can often only be identified as hindsight. Sometimes looking back to past dishes and techniques and problems can lead us to new ways of seeing an ingredient and new inspiration. It is in this constant process of searching, trial and error, and push where Alinea finds its creation.

PASSION

———◆———

by Marcus Samuelsson

PASSION IS WITHOUT a doubt one of the most important keystones of success in the professional restaurant industry. I love what I do to no end, and it was a long journey met with a lot of hard work, but I couldn't have done it without the passion I have for food and for cooking for other people. At every step of my career, passion has been the catalyst to success and the driving force behind my sense of craftsmanship and my eagerness to learn. Passion to me is not only providing unique experiences to those around me through cooking, but also the dedication and hard work behind each moment.

I remember first falling in love with the art of cooking when I was about eight or nine years old while cooking with my uncle. He and I had spent the day fishing at sea, which was hard work but can be a lot of fun. I found it so thrilling to catch the fish, and then it was back to the house to learn how to clean it, filet it, prep it—turning it into the most delicious meal. My grandmother Helga was also hugely influential and taught me the basics of cooking. The whole concept of creating a meal from start to finish—from the earth, to your plate, to your mouth—was magic to me.

My advice to young chefs is wherever your passion for the industry lies, follow that and dig into it. Find what drives you, and dig into it hardcore. Maybe you are attracted to this business because you thrive on the sense of community restaurants bring. Perhaps the opportunity to travel and learn about exotic cuisines is what excites you. Maybe you're the person who has never met a modernist restaurant she didn't like.

Whatever it may be, let it guide you, and find a community that supports and mirrors your passions. Without love for the work you're doing, you won't be able to sustain the pressure and long working hours of a fast-paced kitchen, standing on your feet for hours at a time in front of a hot stove. The industry is always in flux, and the pay for chefs is typically low. You can certainly make good money, but it takes time and hard work. As a young chef I went through all that, and what carried me through each long day was my passion for cooking, hospitality, and working toward something bigger than myself.

I began to understand this when I was opening Red Rooster. I knew I wouldn't be happy opening just any restaurant; to feed my passion for cooking and for my community, it had to live at the intersection of what I loved to cook and what the neighborhood needed. My chefs and staff know how passionate I am about keeping Red Rooster part of the neighborhood. We are always looking to partner with local organizations in Harlem, from the Abyssinian Church to the Harlem Children's Zone. My love for Harlem is what prompted me to start Harlem EatUp!, an entire festival dedicated to showing the people of New York and the world how amazing Harlem is, how much it continues to grow, and that it's a place worth visiting and living in.

I'm devoted to helping the young workers in my restaurant find what gets them excited and start their own paths. In the six years since we opened, I've watched servers become artists and musicians and managers, each successful and confident in their own journey. Watching people who work for me succeed is just another way I continue to give back to the community and feed my passion.

For me, without passion, the environment is not felt. Passion is the heartbeat of my career and what drives me to push myself harder, try new things, ask more questions, and grow as a professional. My passion was reinforced many times while I worked in France, and it profoundly changed my approach to success. I thank Daniel, who has set the bar so high and keeps inspiring us.

TEAMWORK

by Nancy Silverton

You ARE ABOUT to join a select unit, a kitchen brigade. Think of it as joining an elite unit. Maybe even think of it as going into battle. Yes, I know that seems a bit overboard, but if you truly want to be a chef—want that to be your career, your very being even—then it is a life-and-death matter. The life or death of a dream, at least, and we don't want the kitchen to be where your dream dies. Instead, I hope to help you realize your dream.

You are not the general of this battle. That would be the owner (who might also be the chef). You are not the captain, either; that would be the chef de cuisine. You are a solider, a private, the person who fights the battles on the front lines and wins or loses them. You are a cook.

And when you get your third Michelin star, when they want you at all the big food and wine events, you will remain a cook. If you don't love to cook and only want to be a chef—based on what you've seen on cable television—well, let's get this over with right now. Put your dream of being a chef to sleep. Stop reading.

But if the dream is alive, let's get to it. Let's get to that community you are about to move into. The community of your restaurant kitchen.

Never forget that what you do in the kitchen affects everyone. The kitchen succeeds and fails as a team. So it is essential not only to do your job, but to pitch in when the cook to your left is struggling. It might be by taking action, like grabbing the tongs and flipping that rib eye. It might be by offering a few words of encouragement. A simple "You got this" can work magic.

One of my cooks at Osteria Mozza, Kirsten Mayall, compared the extraordinary bond between her fellow line cooks and chef to that within her own family. "It's like my two sisters. Sometimes I can't stand them. They drive me crazy. But, in the end, I'd take a bullet for them."

That lady on pasta to your right, the fella on the grill to your left? They are going to—hopefully only occasionally—drive you batty. Resist the urge to let them wallow, and silently step in. Or simply ask them, with as much sincerity as you can muster, "What can I do?"

My chef at chi SPACCA, Ryan Denicola, values the team player over a cook that thinks he is the next Robuchon. "It's not a luxury," Ryan says. "It's a necessity to work as a team.

It's not about the best cook. People need to be able to set aside their talent for the greater good of the restaurant. The interesting thing is that the people so eager to be the next big chef? That ambition gets in the way of them actually becoming a chef. It holds them back because those people are not good on the team."

Herbert Yuen, a sous at Pizzeria Mozza, tells the new cooks to remember that no task is beneath them. If the walls need scrubbing, scrub them. He also stresses the value of communication. "Communication is underrated. It is one of the keys to a successful kitchen. There is no such thing as overcommunication between cooks."

One last thing. Don't forget that the community of the kitchen extends past those mysterious swinging double doors that lead to that other dimension: the dining room. There are not two teams at an excellent restaurant. The staff in the front of the house are your allies, not the people to blame when a diner's experience falters. One of my best servers, Pat Asanti, whose family hails from Puglia, Italy, told me that the most comforting feeling about our kitchen is knowing that everyone has your back. "No one will let you fail. The Italians call it *la forza de la familia*. The strength of the family."

LOYALTY

Michael Anthony

ONE OF THE most powerful and motivational aspects of working in a professional kitchen is loyalty. It's an idea that is open to interpretation, but if you ask most accomplished chefs, they'll describe feeling some sense of devotion to their own chef or mentor, or even to a partner who helped build their foundational knowledge and taught the lessons that made it possible for them to grow. Finding that mentor is important, but showing them loyalty is even more critical. And it will yield tremendously meaningful benefits.

Over the years I've had so many lasting relationships with great cooks. Sometimes I simply connect with someone—for example, a cook who shows an intense passion that I find familiar and to which I can relate. It's always clear when a cook feels that connection to me as well. These cooks pass up other opportunities because they want to be on my team as long as possible. The more they give to me, the more I want to give back to them. When they do move on, it's rarely the last time we speak. I will work as hard for them as they have for me long after our time of collaborating in the same kitchen is finished.

Loyalty does not mean that once you start with a chef, you are signed on for life or until he or she dismisses you. You don't need to feel guilty about leaving if it's truly not the right fit. But you do owe it a fair shot working at your very best. Joining a new team is a big commitment. I ask cooks who apply for a position in our kitchen if they have organized their lives, time, and personal budgets to allow them to focus completely on the work in front of them. I ask why they are interested in our kitchen since they could choose so many great places to learn. I want to confirm that they understand the power of their choice and feel they are well suited to work within our philosophy and style. I ask the cook, "Why now?" to determine if this is the right moment for him or her to step up to the next phase of his or her career. Mostly, I need to be assured that a potential new hire has the confidence to add to our team's story and feels committed to leaving their station (and our kitchen) better than they found it.

These are questions you can ask yourself as you search for a mentor or a place to plant some roots. I find that the seedling to loyalty is a healthy dose of admiration. Have you ever watched your chef or sous chef and thought, "I want to be like him!"? It sounds elementary but this is often where it begins. You see how your chef works and leads and you admire something about his or her style, technique, mannerisms, sense of humor, discipline, seriousness, or any combination of the sort. I, too, set out to train under the chefs I admired the most, a sentiment that eventually grew to loyalty, which in turn grew to profound friendship. Don't just apply for a job with the most famous chef that comes to your mind. Make sure it's someone you truly admire.

Commitment and admiration are the two facets of loyalty that cooks find obvious and agreeable, but they aren't the only ones. There are also trust and patience, which are not always so easy to swallow.

We know that one person alone doesn't have the power to accomplish the restaurant's needs; doing so takes the entire team, and it requires that team members trust each other and, above all, trust their chef. Working in a professional kitchen can be daunting and frustrating, especially in the heat of service. Arguments and jabs seem inevitable, but the cooks know that my expectations for myself are just as high as the bar I set for them, and I can assure them that I have their backs inside and outside of work. My sincere hope is that I can coach our team to develop the skills and strengths each of them will need to run their own establishments. And perhaps they will far exceed my own abilities in our shared profession. However, during nightly dinner service, they have to put their stock and trust in me.

Each day we try to move forward, and yet some days it doesn't always feel like we accomplish our goal. Patience will pay off. We set realistic, but hard to attain, objectives. Some are concrete, and some are abstract, so there are moments when we may not even realize what we've achieved. To be a loyal part of the crew means to stay the course and follow the leader. We cannot hope to see change overnight, but we can remind ourselves that we are lucky to be able to practice the craft of our choice: making delicious and beautiful food with our hands and to the great pleasure of our guests.

As a young cook, I never thought too intently about loyalty. Yet when I reflect on my career up to this point, it's clear that my allegiances served me well. I certainly hope that the chefs for whom I felt such great admiration and devotion would say that I served them well, too. It's hard to realize it at the time, but when you are a young cook (and you know even less than you think you know), being dependable and steadfast in your passion for learning are the most desirable traits. Loyalty doesn't require that you are handcuffed to a single establishment for an indefinite period of time. It requires that you give 100 percent of yourself every day that you are there. Do this in honor of the chef and the team, and they will be loyal to you for life.

RECIPES:
A SELF-PORTRAIT

———◆———

THERE IS AN expression: "You are what you eat." For a chef it would be closer to the truth to say, "You are what you have cooked." From the first time I scrambled an egg in my parents' kitchen to the many times I have cooked something new and elaborate for a president, top athlete, or movie star, my autobiography is really a collection of the food I have made. I thought it would be unfair in a book that describes food with such passion for me to leave you hungry for more. So from every place where I have lived and cooked, here are some recipes and inspirations that I can truly say I love the most.

ST. PIERRE DE CHANDIEU (HOME)—THE '60s

Chicken Grand-Mère Francine

Everybody's grandmother makes a chicken fricassée, and my grandmother Francine was no exception. She was a sweet lady and cooked at our original family restaurant, Café Boulud. Until she was seven years old she didn't speak French, but, rather, the ancient language of my region, Dauphinois. Mastering this dish means you have learned how to caramelize meat properly, one of the most important techniques for any chef—in the restaurant or at home.

Makes 4 servings

2 tablespoons extra-virgin olive oil
One 3-pound chicken, cut into 8 pieces
Salt and freshly ground white pepper
2 tablespoons unsalted butter
12 cipollini onions, peeled and trimmed
4 shallots, peeled and trimmed
2 heads garlic, cloves separated but not peeled
3 sprigs thyme
4 small Yukon Gold potatoes, peeled and cut into
    1 ½-inch chunks
2 small celery roots, peeled and cut into 1 ½-inch chunks
2 ounces slab bacon, cut into short, thin strips
12 small cremini or oyster mushrooms, cleaned and
    trimmed
2 cups unsalted chicken stock or low-sodium chicken
    broth

    1. Center a rack in the oven and preheat the oven to 375°F.

2. Working over medium-high heat, warm the olive oil in a 12-inch ovenproof sauté pan or skillet—choose one with high sides and a cover. Season the chicken pieces all over with salt and pepper, slip them into the pan, and cook until they are well browned on all sides, about 10 to 15 minutes. Take your time—you want a nice, deep color, and you also want to cook the chicken pieces three-quarters through at this point. When the chicken is deeply golden, transfer it to a platter and keep it in a warm place while you work on the vegetables.

3. Pour off all but 2 tablespoons of the cooking fat from the pan. Lower the heat to medium, add the butter, onions, shallots, garlic, and thyme, and cook, stirring, just until the vegetables start to take on a little color, about 3 minutes. Add the potatoes, celery root, and bacon, and cook 1 to 2 minutes, just to start rendering the bacon fat. Cover the pan and cook another 10 minutes, stirring every 2 minutes.

4. Add the mushrooms, season with salt and pepper, and return the chicken to the pan. Add the chicken stock, bring to a boil, and slide the pan into the oven. Bake, uncovered, for 20 to 25 minutes, or until the chicken is cooked through. Spoon everything onto a warm serving platter or into an attractive casserole.

5. To serve: Bring the chicken to the table, and serve with plenty of pieces of crusty baguette to sop up the sauce. Spread the bread with the soft, caramely garlic, which is easily squeezed out of its skin.

Originally appeared in *Café Boulud Cookbook*, by Daniel Boulud and Dorie Greenspan (Scribner, 1999).

ST. PIERRE DE CHANDIEU—THE '60s

Lamb Barboton

In the wintertime, it was often quite wet and raw at our farm. You needed something to warm up your insides and "stick to your ribs," as they say in America. I always think of my mother making this for Sunday lunch—kind of an Irish stew done Lyonnais style, with the fragrance of *serpolet*, our Provençal wild thyme. My mother would usually serve it with creamed spinach.

Makes 4 to 6 servings

3 pounds boneless lamb shoulder, trimmed of fat and cut into 2-inch chunks

All-purpose flour

Salt and freshly ground black pepper

4 tablespoons unsalted butter

2 large onions (approximately 1 pound), peeled and cut into ½-inch wedges

2 medium leeks (approximately ¼ pound), white and light green parts only, thoroughly washed, cut into ½-inch segments

2 cloves garlic, finely chopped

1 cup dry white wine, preferably a chardonnay

3 pounds Yukon Gold or other yellow-fleshed potatoes, peeled and quartered or cut into 1 ½-inch cubes, reserved in cold water

6 to 8 cups unsalted chicken stock or low-sodium chicken broth

2 sprigs thyme, preferably wild (*serpolet*)

2 sprigs winter savory

1 bay leaf

2 sprigs flat-leaf parsley, leaves only, minced

1. Center a rack in the oven and preheat the oven to 350°F.

2. Lightly dust the lamb with the flour and season with salt and pepper. In an enameled cast-iron Dutch oven or any thick-sided ovenproof roasting dish, warm 2 tablespoons of the butter over medium-high heat. Add the lamb and brown on all sides, 6 to 10 minutes. Add the remaining butter and the onions, leek, and garlic, and sweat the vegetables until they are translucent but still have no color, 8 to 10 minutes. Add the wine, and cook until the liquid reduces by three-quarters. Add the potatoes and stock, making sure that the lamb and vegetables are covered by 1 ½ to 2 inches of liquid. Add the thyme, savory, and bay leaf, and mix well to incorporate. Cover the pan loosely with a lid or with an oiled or buttered piece of parchment paper pricked with a tiny air hole in the center. Return to a boil, and transfer the pot to the preheated oven.

3. Bake the stew for 1 ½ to 2 hours. The lamb should be very tender, and the potatoes should be soft and beginning to break so that they thicken the sauce. Cook a half hour longer, if necessary. Discard the parchment, if using, and the thyme, savory, and bay leaf.

4. Ladle the stew into shallow-rimmed soup bowls and sprinkle with parsley just before serving. Serve with freshly ground pepper and *fleur de sel* on the side.

Originally appeared in *The Pleasures of Slow Food: Celebrating Authentic Traditions, Flavors, and Recipes,* by Corby Kummer (Chronicle Books, 2002).

LYON (THE CAPITAL OF SAUCISSON)—1969

Cervelas Sausage with Pistachios

When I first went to work in Lyon, I lived with my uncle, who was a charcutier. On my day off I would help him out, especially when things got crazy busy in the holiday season. This pistachio sausage was very much in demand that time of year. I kind of think of it as the most extravagant of poached saucissons, especially when you throw in some truffles. They're expensive, I know, but for Christmas, you might not feel too bad about splurging. (You need a sausage stuffer for this recipe.)

Makes six to seven 6-inch sausages

1 pound 6 ounces pork shoulder (or pork cheek meat), cut into 1-inch chunks, well chilled
14 ounces fatback, cut into 1-inch chunks, well chilled
4 teaspoons fine sea salt, plus additional
1 teaspoon freshly ground black pepper, plus additional
Pinch of cayenne pepper
Pinch of sugar
1 tablespoon Calvados, cognac, or brandy
4 to 5 feet calf sausage casing, about 1 ½ to 2 inches in diameter
½ cup shelled pistachio nuts, left whole
2 pounds fingerling potatoes, scrubbed
4 tablespoons unsalted butter
1 tablespoon finely chopped flat-leaf parsley

1. Pass the pork shoulder and fatback through a meat grinder set on the largest holes. (Have your butcher perform this step if you don't own a meat grinder.) Transfer the ground meat to a bowl, and add the 4 teaspoons of salt, 1

teaspoon of black pepper, cayenne, sugar, and Calvados. Mix well, cover with plastic wrap, and refrigerate until needed.

2. Set up the sausage stuffer. Rinse the casings thoroughly, both inside and out, under cold running water. Drain well, and slide nearly the entire length of the casing onto the funnel feeder, scrunching it up as you go. Tie a knot at the free end, and keep it close to the tip of the funnel feeder.

3. Remove the meat from the refrigerator and mix in the pistachio nuts. Turn the machine on, and slowly add some of the stuffing, gently holding and guiding the casing with your free hand so that it fills evenly and firmly. Stuff a 6-inch link, being careful to avoid air bubbles, and then leave a ¼-inch bit of empty casing before making a second link. Repeat with the remaining stuffing, and then detach the long sausage from the machine. Twist the casing at the empty spots or tie it with kitchen string to form distinct and separate links. Tie the ends closed, and cut off any excess casing. Let rest uncovered in the refrigerator for at least 2 days and up to 4 days to allow the casing to dry out a bit as well as to let the meat rest.

4. Using a small needle, prick each sausage link in a few spots. Place them in a pot along with the potatoes, and add enough cold water to cover at least 1 to 2 inches. Bring to a boil, lower the heat, and simmer very gently until the potatoes are tender enough to be pierced with a fork or the point of a knife, 15 to 20 minutes. Keep the sausages and potatoes warm in the cooking liquid until serving.

5. To serve: Drain the sausages and potatoes, and cut the sausages into their separate links. Season the potatoes with salt and pepper, toss them with the butter and parsley, and place them in the center of a warm serving platter. Arrange the sausages on top and serve immediately.

ASCAIN—1971

Trout à la Crème with Chorizo and Peppers

When I took my first trip away from my home region, it was to work in the Pays Basque at a place that had only a coal stove. The mountains were full of rivers. The rivers were full of trout. And at the Hotel Etchola in Ascain, the cellar was full of aging Bayonne hams. Sometimes we would get so busy and the orders would come so fast and furiously that we would throw four or five trout in a pan, poach them with cream and vegetables, and send them out to the dining room, which was full of folks on holiday.

Makes 4 servings

1 green bell pepper, cored, seeded, and deveined
1 red bell pepper, cored, seeded, and deveined
1 yellow bell pepper, cored, seeded, and deveined
1 small onion
1 medium tomato, peeled and seeded
4 ounces dried chorizo
2 cups heavy cream
½ teaspoon *piment d'Espelette* (Espelette pepper)
Four 6- to 8-ounce trout, cleaned and boned
Salt and freshly ground white pepper
8 to 12 slices unsmoked, cured dry ham, such as Jambon
    de Bayonne, Serrano ham, or prosciutto

1. Center a rack in the oven and preheat the oven to 350°F.

2. Cut the green, red, and yellow bell peppers, onion, tomato, and chorizo into strips measuring 1 inch by ¼ inch.

3. In an oval fish pan or a 12-inch ovenproof skillet, mix together the peppers, onion, tomato, chorizo, cream, and *piment d'Espelette,* and bring to a boil. Reduce the heat to a low simmer, and cook until the cream has reduced and thickened, 35 to 40 minutes.

4. Meanwhile, season the inside of each trout with salt and pepper. On a flat work surface, lay 2 to 3 ham slices vertically, slightly overlapping each other. Place the trout across the center of the ham slices. One by one, wrap each piece of ham around the trout. Continue until all four trout are wrapped.

5. Add the fish to the pan, and bake for 30 minutes or until the fish are cooked through. Serve immediately.

VONNAS—1973

Crêpes Vonnassiennes

When I arrived at La Mère Blanc, it was the first time I worked in a restaurant with women in the kitchen. Georges Blanc's mother was there on weekends, and there were also two women in the kitchen whose only job was to oversee some of the traditional dishes: Frog's Legs, Poulet à la Crème, and Crêpes Vonnassiennes. Truly nobody could approach the magic touch that Marie, one of the chefs, had with this dish.

Makes about 4 dozen crêpes

1 pound Yukon Gold or Idaho potatoes, peeled and
　　roughly chopped
3 tablespoons milk
3 tablespoons all-purpose flour
3 large eggs
4 large egg whites
2 tablespoons crème fraîche
Salt and freshly ground white pepper
Clarified butter

1. Put the potatoes in a large pot of salted cold water, bring to a boil, and cook until the potatoes are tender enough to be pierced with a fork or the point of a knife, about 15 minutes. Drain the potatoes and return them to the pot. Set the pot over medium heat and, shaking the pot to keep the potatoes from sticking, cook just until the potatoes are dry, 1 to 2 minutes. Remove the pot from the heat, and spoon the potatoes into a potato ricer or a food mill fitted with the fine blade. Push the potatoes through the ricer

or food mill into a large bowl. Stir in the milk, and let the mixture cool to room temperature. Using a whisk, stir in the flour, eggs, egg whites, and crème fraîche, mixing well after each addition. The mixture should have the consistency of a thick custard. Season to taste with salt and pepper.

2. Warm 1 tablespoon butter in a large nonstick skillet over high heat. When the butter is hot, spoon into the pan as many 2-inch circles of batter as will fit. Cook until golden brown, 20 to 30 seconds. Flip the crêpes over and cook on the second side until golden brown, 20 to 30 seconds. Transfer the crêpes to a paper towel–lined plate. Repeat with the remaining batter, adding butter to the pan as needed.

3. Serve warm as a side dish, or sprinkle with confectioner's sugar and serve as a dessert.

With thanks to Georges Blanc and *Larousse Gastronomique*.

MOUGINS—1975

Filet of Beef with Raisin and Pepper Sauce

A glorified steak au poivre. The first time I tried it was with Vergé. It was sweet, spicy, beefy, and what I loved most was that it wasn't the classic creamy steak au poivre. The sauce is more like one you might serve with game. In fact, you can apply this recipe to venison or bison as well as beef.

For the roasted fingerling potatoes:

1 tablespoon extra-virgin olive oil
1 pound fingerling potatoes, scrubbed and halved lengthwise
Salt and freshly ground white pepper
1 tablespoon unsalted butter
1 clove garlic, crushed
1 sprig thyme

Warm the oil in a large skillet over high heat. When the oil is hot, add the potatoes, and season with salt and pepper. Brown evenly on all sides, turning as needed. Reduce the heat to medium, add the butter, garlic, and thyme, and cook until the potatoes are tender. Discard the garlic and thyme. Set the potatoes aside and keep warm.

For the sautéed spinach:

1 ½ teaspoons unsalted butter
1 ½ pounds spinach, stemmed and tough center veins removed
2 cloves garlic, crushed
Salt and freshly ground white pepper

Melt the butter in a large skillet over high heat. Add the spinach and garlic, and season to taste with salt and pepper. Toss until the spinach is tender but still bright green, about 5 minutes. Discard the garlic and drain off any liquid remaining in the pan. Set aside and keep warm.

For the beef and sauce:

½ cup golden raisins
¼ cup cognac or Armagnac
1 teaspoon coarsely crushed whole pink peppercorns
1 teaspoon coarsely crushed whole green peppercorns
½ teaspoon coarsely crushed whole black peppercorns
½ teaspoon coarsely crushed Szechuan peppercorns
1 whole Jamaican peppercorn, crushed
One 1 ½-pound beef tenderloin, trimmed of fat and cut into 4 slices
Coarse salt
4 tablespoons unsalted butter
⅓ cup unsalted beef stock or low-sodium beef broth

1. Bring 2 cups of water to a boil in a small saucepan. Add the raisins, reduce the heat, and simmer for 5 minutes. Drain the raisins and run them under cold running water. Drain again. Place the raisins in a small bowl, and pour the cognac over them. Cover the bowl with plastic wrap and refrigerate overnight.

2. Combine the peppercorns. Season the meat with the coarse salt, and press the peppercorns into the meat. Warm 2 tablespoons of the butter in a large skillet over medium heat. Slip the filets into the pan and cook for 4 to 5 minutes on each side for medium-rare. Transfer the meat to a platter and keep warm.

3. Drain the fat from the skillet. Add the raisins and cognac to the pan, return the pan to high heat, and bring to a boil. Cook until the liquid is reduced by half. Add the beef stock, reduce the heat, and simmer for 2 minutes. Cut the remaining 2 tablespoons of butter into very small pieces. Gradually add the butter to the sauce, stirring constantly. Season to taste with salt. Add the meat to the pan and baste with the sauce.

4. To serve: Divide the meat and sauce among four warm dinner plates. Serve with the fingerling potatoes and spinach.

Adapted from Roger Vergé's original recipe as it appeared in *Roger Vergé's Cuisine of the South of France* (William Morrow and Co., 1980).

COPENHAGEN—1977

Chestnut-Crusted Venison Loin

In Denmark, especially during hunting season, we served a lot of game. Elk and venison were particular favorites. In the restaurant we often served venison with huckleberry sauce. The chestnut-crusted loin is an idea that came to me years later, but I think of it as an homage to my time in Denmark.

Makes 6 servings

For the crust:

¾ pound peeled fresh chestnuts (from about 1 ¼ pounds in the shell), or ¾ pound dry-packed bottled or vacuum-sealed peeled fresh chestnuts

1. Break each chestnut into a few pieces, and spread them out on a baking sheet. Allow the pieces to dry overnight in a warm place—inside an oven with a pilot light is perfect.

2. The next day, place the chestnuts in the work bowl of a food processor, and pulse until they break into ¼-inch chunks. Sift the chestnuts, reserving the larger pieces that remain in the sieve, and discarding the powder or saving it for another use. Transfer the pieces to a plate and keep close at hand.

For the marinade:

1 teaspoon grated orange zest
½ cup freshly squeezed orange juice
2 tablespoons extra-virgin olive oil
1 teaspoon ground cinnamon

½ teaspoon freshly grated nutmeg
¼ teaspoon ground star anise
¼ teaspoon whole black peppercorns
2 cloves garlic, peeled and crushed
1 sprig thyme
Two 1 ½-pound venison loins, trimmed

Mix all the marinade ingredients together in a shallow pan, then roll the venison around in the marinade to coat. Cover the pan tightly with plastic wrap, and refrigerate for at least 4 hours, or preferably overnight, turning the meat a few times during this period.

For the rutabaga:

Zest from ½ orange (pith removed), cut into very thin
    strands
2 tablespoons extra-virgin olive oil
1 large rutabaga, peeled and cut into ½-inch cubes
Large pinch of ground cinnamon
Small pinch of freshly grated nutmeg
Small pinch of ground star anise
1 clove garlic, peeled
1 sprig thyme
Salt and freshly ground pepper
1 cup unsalted chicken stock or low-sodium chicken broth

1. Put the orange zest in a small pot of water and bring to a boil. Boil 2 minutes; drain and set aside.

2. Warm the olive oil in a large sauté pan or skillet over medium heat. Add the rutabaga, spices, garlic, thyme, and salt and pepper to taste, and cook, stirring, for 5 minutes, without letting the rutabaga color. Add the chicken stock, bring to a boil, cover the pan, and lower the heat to keep the

liquid at a simmer. Braise the rutabaga for 15 minutes, or until it can be pierced easily with the tip of a knife.

3. Remove the cover and cook the rutabaga, stirring and turning it gently, until it is glazed and the liquid in the pan has evaporated. Discard the garlic and thyme. Just before serving, stir in the orange zest. (The rutabaga can be made several hours ahead, kept covered in the refrigerator, then warmed over gentle heat before serving; stir in the zest at serving time.)

To cook the venison:

Salt and freshly ground white pepper
2 large eggs
1 large egg yolk
3 tablespoons all-purpose flour
¼ cup extra-virgin olive oil

1. Center a rack in the oven and preheat the oven to 425°F.

2. Remove the venison from the marinade and discard the marinade. Pat the meat dry with paper towels and season with salt and white pepper. In a pan or dish long enough to accommodate the venison loins, beat together the eggs and yolk. Dust one side of each loin with flour, shake off the excess, and dip that side into the egg mixture and then into the chestnuts.

3. Heat the olive oil in a roasting pan over medium heat. When the oil is hot, add the venison, chestnut-side down, and cook for about 2 minutes. Turn the loins over and place the roasting pan in the oven. Roast the venison 10 to 12 minutes, until medium-rare. Pull the pan from the oven, and transfer the loins to a warm platter. (You will use the

roasting pan with the drippings to make the sauce.) Set the meat aside in a warm place while you make the sauce.

For the sauce:

1 small shallot, peeled, trimmed, finely chopped, rinsed, and dried
2 teaspoons coarsely crushed black pepper
1 teaspoon grated orange zest
4 teaspoons balsamic vinegar
1 cup dry red wine
1 teaspoon sugar
1 ½ cups unsalted beef stock or low-sodium beef broth
Salt and freshly ground black pepper
2 teaspoons unsalted butter

1. Remove as much grease from the liquid in the roasting pan as possible, and place the pan over medium heat. Add the shallot and cook, stirring, just until translucent. Add the pepper and orange zest, sauté for a minute more, and then deglaze the pan with the balsamic vinegar, cooking and stirring until the vinegar just about evaporates. Add the red wine and cook down again until the pan is almost dry. Add the sugar and beef stock, and cook at a boil until the liquid is reduced by half. Taste, and add salt and pepper as needed. Remove the pan from the heat, and swirl the butter into the sauce.

2. To serve: Slice the loins into 12 to 16 slices, and arrange them attractively on a warm platter. Moisten with the sauce, and serve with the spiced rutabaga.

Originally appeared in *Café Boulud Cookbook*, by Daniel Boulud and Dorie Greenspan (Scribner, 1999).

LES PRÉS D'EUGÉNIE—1978

Caramelized Pears with Puff Pastry and Pear Cream

So simple in its ingredients yet requiring all the skills of the pastry chef: the flaky crust, the sweet poached fruit, the fluffy and deeply flavored cream. Here Guérard, the gastronomic chef, returns to the pastry kitchen, where he started. Simple. Unforgettable.

Makes 6 servings

For the poached pears:
1 moist, plump vanilla bean
¾ cup sugar
Freshly squeezed juice of 1 lemon
3 ripe Bosc pears

Cut the vanilla bean in half lengthwise and, using the back of the knife blade, scrape the pulp out of the pod. Put the pulp and pod, sugar, and lemon juice in a medium saucepan with 1 quart of water and bring to a boil. Lower the heat to keep the liquid at a simmer, peel the pears (you don't want to do this earlier—they'll darken), and add the whole pears to the pot. Cook the pears at a gentle simmer just until they can be pierced with the tip of a knife, 20 to 30 minutes. Remove the pot from the heat, and allow the pears to cool in the poaching liquid. (The pears can be made 3 days ahead and should be kept in their poaching syrup for storage in the refrigerator. Drain the fruit before using.)

For the pastry cream:

1 moist, plump vanilla bean
2 cups whole milk

½ cup sugar
4 large egg yolks
3 tablespoons all-purpose flour
3 tablespoons cornstarch

1. Line a deep, rimmed plate with plastic wrap, leaving ample overhang. Cut the vanilla bean in half lengthwise and, using the back of the knife blade, scrape the pulp out of the pod.

2. Pour the milk into a medium saucepan. Stir in ¼ cup of the sugar. Add the vanilla bean, both pod and pulp, and bring to the boil. While the milk is coming to a boil, vigorously whisk the yolks and the remaining ¼ cup sugar together in a bowl until the mixture turns pale, then whisk in the flour and cornstarch.

3. Whisking continuously, very gradually add half the hot milk to the egg mixture. Pour into the saucepan and, still whisking, cook over medium heat until the pastry cream thickens and starts to boil. Allow the pastry cream to boil for 30 seconds, while constantly whisking, then scrape it onto the plastic-lined plate. Smooth the top of the cream with a rubber spatula, and cover the cream with the overhanging plastic wrap (or another sheet of plastic). Press the plastic against the surface of the pastry cream; you don't want the cream to come in contact with air and develop a skin. Transfer the plate to the refrigerator until the cream is chilled. Remove the vanilla bean when the cream is cold. (The pastry cream can be made up to 2 days in advance and kept covered in an airtight container in the refrigerator. This recipe will make more cream than you need.)

For the puff pastry:

1 sheet (about ½ pound) frozen puff pastry, thawed
1 egg, lightly beaten
Confectioners' sugar

1. Center a rack in the oven and preheat the oven to 425°F.

2. Cut the puff pastry into six rectangles measuring 2 by 1 ½ inches each, and transfer to a baking sheet. Very gently brush the pastry rectangles with the beaten egg, being careful not to let the egg run over the edges. Bake for 10 to 12 minutes until golden brown. Remove the baking sheet from the oven. Preheat the broiler. Liberally dust the tops of the puff pastry with confectioners' sugar. Broil for 30 seconds to 1 minute—watch closely—just until the sugar has melted and caramelized. Transfer the rectangles to a wire rack and let cool. Carefully split the top quarter of each rectangle from the bottom and set aside.

Assembly:

1 cup heavy cream
2 tablespoons pear brandy (Poire William)
Granulated sugar

1. Preheat the broiler.

2. Remove the pears from the poaching syrup with a slotted spoon. Carefully cut each pear in half lengthwise and core it. Trim the pear halves so that they are the same size as the puff pastry rectangles, and thinly slice them crosswise. Reserve the pear scraps. Transfer the sliced pear halves to a lightly buttered baking sheet. Press on each pear half to fan

the slices toward the wider end. Sprinkle a liberal amount of sugar over the pears, and broil 1 to 2 minutes—watch them closely—until the sugar is golden brown. (You can also caramelize the sugar with a blow torch or salamander.)

3. Coarsely chop the reserved pear scraps. Using a whisk, whip the heavy cream to medium peaks in a medium bowl. Whisk together ½ cup of the pastry cream and the brandy in a separate mixing bowl. Gently fold the whipped cream and the chopped pears into the pastry cream/brandy mixture to make the pear cream. Spoon about 2 tablespoons of the pear cream into the bottom of each puff pastry rectangle. Cover with the puff pastry top. Spread a thin layer of the plain pastry cream on top of the puff pastry. Using a spatula, arrange the caramelized pears on top. Serve immediately.

Adapted from Michel Guérard's original recipe, as it appeared in *Les Recettes Originales de Michel Guérard* (Éditions Robert Laffert, 1978).

NEW YORK, LE CIRQUE—1987

Bollito Misto

The first dish I learned when I went to Le Cirque, this is a true "feast for the village." I can still envision the steam every time we opened the terrine and can hear the inevitable "oohs" and "ahs" from the patrons. It takes a lot to get a Frenchman (especially a chef) to admit that another nation makes a better pot-au-feu, but on a *buon giorno*, it's hard to beat a bollito misto.

Makes 12 to 16 servings

For the salsa verde:

12 anchovies, finely chopped
6 tablespoons capers, rinsed, drained, and finely chopped
4 cloves garlic, finely chopped
1 bunch flat-leaf parsley, leaves only, finely chopped
¼ bunch basil, leaves only, finely chopped
¾ cup to 1 cup extra-virgin olive oil

Combine all the ingredients. (The sauce can be made 1 day in advance.)

For the bollito misto (should be made 1 day in advance):

2 pig's feet, each cut into 6 segments (ask your butcher to do this)
One 2-pound slab bacon
1 calf's head, deboned, cut in half, rolled, and tied (ask your butcher to do this)
1 veal shank, trimmed (ask your butcher to do this)
1 short rib
24 Yukon Gold potatoes, peeled

12 turnips, trimmed

12 large carrots, trimmed and cut in half

6 onions, peeled and studded with cloves

6 leeks, split lengthwise, washed and trimmed

2 bunches celery, trimmed and each stalk cut in half

2 bay leaves

1 tablespoon whole black peppercorns

1 fresh veal tongue

One 3-pound chicken, trussed

12 zampones or cotechinos, casings pricked with a fork

Salt and freshly ground black pepper

Italian mustard fruits (*mostarda di frutta*), cut into ¼-inch
   dice (for serving)

1. In the largest pot you have, place the pig's feet, bacon, calf's head, veal shank, short rib, potatoes, turnips, carrots, onions, leeks, celery, bay leaves, and peppercorns. Add enough water to cover all the ingredients, about 4 to 5 gallons. Bring to a boil. Lower the heat and simmer, skimming the surface regularly, for 45 minutes. Check the potatoes, and if they are tender enough to be pierced with the point of a knife, remove them and place them in a large bowl.

2. Continue to cook for 1 hour and 15 minutes, skimming the surface regularly. Transfer the remaining vegetables to a large bowl and set aside. Add the tongue and cook for 1 hour.

3. Remove the pig's feet, bacon, and calf's head. Add the chicken and cook for 30 minutes.

4. Add the sausages and cook for 30 minutes.

5. Check to see if the chicken is tender and cooked through. Remove the meats from the broth. Strain the broth through a fine-mesh sieve, and season to taste with salt and

pepper, if needed. Refrigerate the meats and broth separately overnight. (The meats will be easier to slice when cold.)

6. To serve: Slice the meats. Rewarm the meats and the vegetables in the broth. Arrange the meats and vegetables on a large, warm serving platter to be passed around. Place the broth in a soup tureen to be passed around. Serve with the salsa verde and the Italian mustard fruits.

NEW YORK, DANIEL—2000

Pancetta-Wrapped Tuna with Potato-Ramp Purée

A rustic yet majestic dish. I made it for Bill Clinton when he spent a weekend in East Hampton. I have yet to find someone who doesn't like this dish a lot, and I put it on the menu at least once a season. I suppose my favorite time, though, is in the spring, when we get wild ramps from the Hudson Valley. In a way, this recipe is a summing up of where my career has taken me: the rare tuna is very *au courant* and New York-ish, and the pancetta is like the charcuterie I used to help my uncle make all those years ago.

Makes 6 servings

For the tuna:

8 to 10 ounces slab pancetta, thinly sliced, or an equal
  amount of sliced bacon
1 ¼ pounds tuna loin, cut like a roast, approximately 6
  inches long, 1 ½ inches high, and 1 ½ inches wide
Salt and freshly ground black pepper

Spread a piece of plastic wrap on the counter, and on it lay out the slices of pancetta (or bacon) vertically, so that each slice overlaps its neighboring slice just a bit. Season the tuna very lightly with salt and pepper (remember, the pancetta or bacon is already salty), and place it crosswise down the middle of the pancetta strips. One by one, wrap each piece of pancetta around the tuna, pressing the pancetta gently against the tuna and keeping the rows even. Secure the pancetta by tying the roast at 1 inch intervals with kitchen twine, just as you would a meat roast. Wrap the tuna in plastic wrap, and refrigerate it while you prepare the potatoes.

For the potatoes and ramps:

1 ¾ pounds potatoes, preferably fingerlings, peeled and cut
    into ½-inch pieces
¾ cup whole milk
8 tablespoons (1 stick) unsalted butter, cut into 8 pieces
3 ounces ramps or 3 ounces scallion greens (from about
    4 to 5 ounces scallions), trimmed and washed
1 bunch Italian parsley, leaves only
4 tablespoons extra-virgin olive oil
1 clove garlic, finely chopped (optional)
Salt and freshly ground white pepper

1. Put the potatoes in a large pot of salted cold water, bring to a boil, and cook until the potatoes are tender enough to be pierced with the point of a knife, about 15 minutes.

2. While the potatoes are cooking, bring the milk and butter to a boil in a small saucepan. When the mixture boils and the butter melts, turn off the heat; keep the mixture warm until you're ready to purée the potatoes.

3. When the potatoes are cooked through, drain them and return them to the pot. Set the pot over medium heat and, shaking the pot to keep the potatoes from sticking, cook just until the potatoes are dry, a minute or two. Remove the pot from the heat, and spoon the potatoes into a potato ricer or a food mill fitted with the fine blade. Push the potatoes through the ricer or food mill into a large bowl. In a slow, steady stream, add the hot milk and butter,

stirring the liquid into the potatoes with a wooden spoon. Press a piece of plastic wrap against the surface of the potatoes, and set the bowl aside in a warm place, or keep the potatoes warm in a covered heatproof bowl set over a pan of simmering water.

4. Bring a small pot of water to a boil. Toss the ramps or scallion greens into the pot, and boil for 3 to 4 minutes, until tender. Scoop the ramps or scallions out of the pot with a slotted spoon (keep the boiling water over the heat) and run them under cold water to cool; dry them well. Toss the parsley into the boiling water and cook for 2 minutes. Drain the parsley and run it under cold water. When the parsley is cool, dry it as well.

5. Warm 1 tablespoon of the olive oil in a medium sauté pan or skillet over medium heat. If you're using garlic, add it to the pan and sauté until it is tender but not colored, about 2 minutes. Toss in the ramps or scallions and cook, stirring, for 3 minutes. Scrape the ingredients into the container of a small processor or a blender. Add the drained and dried parsley and the remaining 3 tablespoons of olive oil, and whir, scraping down the sides of the container as needed, until you have a smooth purée. Stir the purée into the potatoes, season with salt and pepper, cover again, and keep warm while you cook the tuna.

To finish:

3 tablespoons unsalted butter
6 ounces chanterelles, trimmed and cleaned (halved or
      quartered if large)
1 tablespoon finely chopped shallots, rinsed and dried
Salt and freshly ground white pepper

¼ cup sherry vinegar
¼ cup dry white wine
¼ cup homemade unsalted chicken stock, or store-bought
 low-sodium chicken broth
2 tablespoons finely chopped chives

1. Center a rack in the oven and preheat the oven to
350°F.

2. Warm 1 tablespoon of the butter in a large, ovenproof
sauté pan or skillet over medium heat; when it's hot, slip
the tuna into the pan. Sear the tuna for about 2 minutes
on each of its four sides, then slide the pan into the oven
for 5 minutes. (After 5 minutes in the oven, the tuna will
be warm and rare-cooked on the outside but not colored
anywhere else. If this is too rare for you, increase the tuna's
time in the oven by 1 to 2 minutes, and you'll have medium
tuna.) Lift the tuna out of the pan and onto a warm serving
platter (don't discard the cooking fat).

3. Pour off half the cooking fat from the pan, return
the pan to the stovetop, turn the heat to medium-low, and
toss in the chanterelles. Cover the pan and cook the mushrooms until they're almost tender but not colored, 3 to 5
minutes. Add the shallots, season with salt and pepper, and
cook another minute or so to soften the shallots. Pour in
the vinegar, and allow it to reduce by three-quarters. Add
the white wine, bring the mixture to the boil, and allow the
wine to cook away. Add the chicken stock. Cook until the
stock is reduced by half, then remove the pan from the heat
and swirl in the remaining 2 tablespoons of butter, a small
piece at a time. (The idea is to melt the butter slowly so that
it forms an emulsion.) Sprinkle in the chives.

4. To serve: Cut the tuna into 12 slices (this is done most easily with an electric knife or a very sharp, long, thin-bladed knife). On each of six warm dinner plates, center a scoop of potatoes, lean two slices of tuna against the potatoes, and surround with chanterelles and sauce.

Originally appeared in *Café Boulud Cookbook*, by Daniel Boulud and Dorie Greenspan (Scribner, 1999).

ACKNOWLEDGMENTS

THIS PROJECT BEGAN as a small update to a book I wrote almost fifteen years ago, but in revising it I realized there was (and still is) so much more to say about the work and life of a young chef. Many friends and colleagues who share the same values have helped me to develop and write this new edition, which, hopefully, will continue to motivate young cooks at all levels to achieve success and happiness. I am grateful to those who have made a contribution, either directly with their words and efforts or by inspiring my own. For sure, the list of people who support me daily is even longer than it was a decade ago. Here are just a few.

First and foremost to Peter Kaminsky, for the countless hours he spent patiently recording my ideas and guiding my thoughts. His humor, style, and in-depth knowledge of our industry allowed me to convey my views clearly and in a voice I could always call my own.

A special thanks to my Culinary Manager, Mary Kirk Goeldner, who helped with much of the rewriting project. Her patience and ability to translate my handwritten notes and scribbles were invaluable.

To the generous people at Basic Books who created the first edition, and especially the talented team tasked to the second edition: Melissa Veronesi, Melissa Raymond, Katherine Haigler, Lara Heimert, Alia Massoud, and my copy editor, Kelley Blewster.

To all the chefs who tirelessly maintain the standards in my restaurants, but especially Corporate Chefs Fabrizzio Salerni and Olivier Muller, who manage to juggle the dynamic demands of the business, food, and personnel at our properties worldwide; to Jean-Francois Bruel, Eddy Leroux, and Ghaya Oliveira, who are at the helm of my flagship, DANIEL; to Aaron Bludorn and Ashley Brauze at Café Boulud, Travis Swikard at Boulud Sud, Alexander Burger and Anna McGorman at Bar Boulud, and Christopher Stam at DB Bistro Moderne.

To all my chefs outside New York who bring talent and passion for French cuisine to their cities: Sylvain Assie in Toronto, Riccardo Bertolino in Montreal, Rick Mace in Palm Beach, Clark Bowen in Miami, Thomas Piat in London, Michael Denk in Boston, Jonathan Kinsella in Singapore, and Nicholas Tang in Washington, DC.

As no kitchen staff could shine without the arduous efforts of the front of the house, I thank Pierre Siue, Dominique Paulin, and Samantha Whitlam, my operations directors, who oversee all aspects of service in multiple locations.

To Brett Traussi and Michael Lawrence, Chief Operations Officer and Executive Director of Operations, who have been with me since the early 90s and who make the whole machine run. Their stamina and drive keep us pushing toward our common goal: excellence in hospitality.

To my partners, Lili Lynton and the Smilow family, and my financial directors, Marcel Doron and Brian Diamond, for insisting we each give our very best every day.

To Evyn Block, my Director of Public Relations, who makes sure we all stay focused, creative, and connected.

To the entire Dinex Group staff in accounting, public relations, marketing, human resources, purchasing, and administration, for keeping us staffed, organized, engaged, and relevant.

To Young Yun, Jaimie Chew, and Tehani Levin, the directors of the foundation Ment'or BKB, for their efforts to create great opportunities for young chefs and for Team USA on behalf of myself, Thomas Keller, and Jerome Bocuse.

To my multilingual, multiskilled administrative assistants, Anna Hahn and Juliette Ten, who are undoubtedly the most patient and organized of the team. They manage my communications, busy schedule, devices, transportation, and general comfort, and I owe them much gratitude.

To all the young chefs who have worked in my kitchens and have given their dedication, their energy, their willingness to learn. To the sous chefs, cooks, bakers, externs, *stagiaires,* and culinary students who have worked, for five days or five years, as part of my brigade: I am thankful for your loyalty and commitment. It is so very rewarding to observe those of you who have passed through my doors and gone on to create and sustain your own extraordinary successes—in the United States and around the world. There is no greater joy as a chef or mentor than knowing I have had some small influence on your careers. You make me proud and remind me why I am here in the first place.

To my entire restaurant staff: no chef operates in a vacuum. It takes teamwork from every member of the front and back of the house. You are all part of that which keeps my wheels turning and my dream possible. Every phone answered, every dish washed, and every delivery inspected is vital.

To American cooking schools, who have transformed the landscape of culinary education over the last few decades. Their efforts have increased the respect and understanding of our profession in this country.

Of course, to my mentors, Gerard Nandron, Georges Blanc, Roger Vergé, Michel Guérard, and Sirio Maccioni, for giving me the tools I needed and the lessons I learned.

When you are a chef you will become part of a great community of other chefs who are your buddies, but whom you will also greatly respect for their perspective on our craft. For this edition I asked a few of mine to contribute essays. I would like to thank Grant Achatz, Dominique Ansel, Michael Anthony, Gavin Kaysen, Corey Lee, Barbara Lynch, Eric Ripert, Marcus Samuelsson, Nancy Silverton, and, from my current team, Jean-Francois Bruel and Eddy Leroux, for giving their time away from their own businesses to help me guide and influence young chefs today.

Finally, to my wife, Katherine, my two daughters, Alix and Georgiana, and my son, Julien, for their love, support, and patience. And to my parents, Julien and Marie Boulud, as well as my late Grandmère Francine, with whom my whole story begins and to whom I will always be grateful for their encouragement and support.

DANIEL BOULUD is considered one of America's leading culinary authorities and one of the most revered French chefs in New York, his home since 1982. Daniel was born in France in 1955 and raised on his family's farm near Lyon. He got his first restaurant job at the age of fourteen. After being nominated as a candidate for best cooking apprentice in France, Daniel went on to train under renowned chefs Roger Vergé, Georges Blanc, and Michel Guérard. He then moved to the United States, where his first position was as Chef to the European Commission in Washington, DC. From 1986 to 1992, he served as Executive Chef at New York's famed Le Cirque. He opened his flagship restaurant, DANIEL, on Manhattan's Upper East Side in 1993. Daniel is now Chef-Owner of fourteen restaurants around the world; outside New York, his cooking can be found in London, Singapore, Toronto, Montréal, Miami, Palm Beach, Washington, DC, and Boston. Boulud is the author of nine cookbooks; the recipient of multiple James Beard Foundation awards, including Outstanding Chef and Outstanding Restaurateur; and winner of the Culinary Institute of America's Chef of the Year Award (2011) and the World's 50 Best Restaurants Lifetime Achievement Award (2015). Boulud was named a Chevalier de la Légion d'Honneur by the French government in March 2006 in recognition of his contributions to the advancement of French culture. He has been a generous supporter and Co-President of Citymeals on Wheels for more than two decades, and is Chairman of the Ment'or BKB Foundation.